Galloping Cookie Dough

Written & Illustrated
by B. K. Hixson

Galactic Cookie Dough

Copyright © 2003
First Printing • June 2003
B. K. Hixson

Published by Loose in the Lab, Inc.
9462 South 560 West
Sandy, Utah 84070

www.looseinthelab.com

Library of Congress Cataloging-in-Publication Data:

Hixson, B. K.
    Galactic Cookie Dough/B. K. Hixson
    p.   cm.-(Loose in the Lab Science Series)

    Includes index
    ISBN 1-931801-06-1
    1. Astronomy experiments-juvenile literature. [1
Astronomy experiments 2. Experiments] I. B. K. Hixson
II. Loose in the Lab III. Title IV. Series
QB 46.H 363   2003
152.14

Printed in the United States of America
We need more fruitcakes!

Dedication

For Pooh

Who says the stars don't conspire to meddle in the lives of mere mortals and work their magic on the intergalactic travelers who happen to congregate in this corner of the galaxy? Here's to a long and happy dance while we are here and an extended tour of the stars when the music starts up again.

Hugs & Kisses,

Bryce

Acknowledgments

Getting a book out for public consumption is far from a one-man job. There are lots of thank-yous to be doodled out and, at the risk of leaving someone out, we attempt to do that on this page. In terms of my astronomy education, I would have to say that lying on my back at Camp Baldwin, as a Boy Scout, was the first time that I was formally introduced to the wonder of the heavens. It was on those summer nights that I learned not only about constellations and the legends that they inspired but also about things called red giants, crab nebulae, and the immense distances between seemingly crowded clusters of stars. I still get caught gazing at the grandeur of it all and for a moment, feel completely insignificant. But then a hot coal usually launches itself onto my bare leg and I pop back into reality at the speed of burning hair.

As for my educational outlook, the hands-on perspective, and the use of humor in the classroom, Dr. Fox, my senior professor at Oregon State University, gets the credit for shaping my educational philosophy while simultaneously recognizing that even at the collegiate level, we were on to something a little different. He did his very best to encourage, nurture, and support me while I was getting basketloads of opposition for being willing to swim upstream. There were also several colleagues who helped to channel my enthusiasm during those early, formative years of teaching: Dick Bishop, Dick Hinton, Dee Strange, Connie Ridgway, and Linda Zimmermann. Thanks for your patience, friendship, and support.

Next up are all the folks who get to do the dirty work that makes the final publication look so polished but very rarely get the credit they deserve. Our resident graphics guru, Kris Barton, gets a nod for scanning and cleaning the artwork you find on these pages, as well as putting together the graphics that make up the cover. A warm Yankee yahoo to Eve Laubner, our editor, who passes her comments on so that Kathleen Hixson and Eve Laubner (once again) can take turns simultaneously proofreading the text while mocking my writing skills.

Once we have a finished product, it has to be printed so that the good folks at Delta Education—Gary Facente, Louisa Walker, Selina Gerow, and the whole gang—can market and ship the books, collect the money, and send us a couple of nickels. It's a short thank-you for some very important jobs.

Mom and Dad, as always, get the end credits. Thanks for the education, encouragement, and love. And for Kathy and the kids—Porter, Shelby, Courtney, and Aubrey—hugs and kisses.

Repro Rights

There is very little about this book that is truly formal, but at the insistence of our wise and esteemed counsel, let us declare: *No part of this book may be reproduced or utilized in any form or by any means, electronic or mechanical, including photocopying, recording, or by any information storage and retrieval system, without permission in writing from the publisher.* That would be us.

More Legal Stuff

Official disclaimer for you aspiring scientists and lab groupies. This is a hands-on science book. By the very intent of its design, you will be directed to use common, nontoxic household items in a safe and responsible manner to avoid injury to yourself and others who are present while you are pursuing your quest for knowledge and enlightenment in the world of astronomy. Just make sure that you have a fire blanket handy and a wall-mounted video camera to corroborate your story.

If, for some reason, perhaps even beyond your own control, you have an affinity for disaster, we wish you well. *But we in no way take any responsibility for any injury that is incurred to any person using the information provided in this book or for any damage to personal property or effects that is directly or indirectly a result of the suggested activities contained herein.* Translation: You're on your own. Watch your fingers so you don't smudge the telescope, and if any aliens ask, say, "No, I don't want to see your schmadiddle whacker, thank you very much."

Less Formal Legal Stuff

If you happen to be a home schooler or very enthusiastic school teacher, please feel free to make copies of this book for your classroom or personal family use—one copy per student, up to 35 students. If you would like to use an experiment from this book for a presentation to your faculty or school district, we would be happy to oblige. Just give us a whistle and we will send you a release for the particular lab activity you wish to use. Please contact us at the address below. Thanks.

Special Requests
Loose in the Lab, Inc.
9462 South 560 West
Sandy, Utah 84070

Table of Contents

The National Content Standards (Grades K-4)
• *The sun, moon, stars, clouds, birds, and airplanes all have properties, locations, and movements that can be observed and described.*
• *The sun provides the light and heat necessary to maintain the temperature of the Earth.*
• *Objects in the sky have patterns of movement. The sun, for example, appears to move across the sky in the same way every day, but its path changes slowly over the seasons. The moon moves across the sky on a daily basis much like the sun. The observable shape of the moon changes from day to day in a cycle that lasts about a month.*

The National Content Standards (Grades 5-8)
• *The Earth is the third planet from the sun in a system that includes the moon, the sun, eight other planets and their moons, and smaller objects, such as asteroids and comets. The sun, an average star, is the central and largest body in the solar system.*
• *Most objects in the solar system are in regular and predictable motion. These motions explain such phenomenon as the day, the year, phases of the moon, and eclipses.*
• *Gravity is the force that keeps planets in orbit around the sun and governs the rest of the motion in the solar system. Gravity alone holds us to the Earth's surface and explains the phenomenon of the tides.*
• *The sun is the major source of energy for phenomena on the Earth's surface, such as growth of plants, winds, ocean currents, and the water cycle. Seasons result from variations in the amount of the sun's energy hitting the surface, due to the tilt of the Earth's rotation on its axis and the length of the day.*

The 7 Big Ideas About Astronomy & Corresponding Labs

1. The sun is a medium-sized star at the center of our solar system. It radiates a spectrum of electromagnetic energy out into the universe.

2. In addition to the sun, our solar system is composed of nine planets that orbit our star.

Even More Contents

3. The movements of the sun, Earth, and moon are predictable and regular. These movements produce daily, monthly, and annual phenomena.

4. The moon and Earth have many characteristics—some that are shared with other planets and moons and some that are unique.

5. The sun is a star that has all of the characteristics of other stars in our universe.

6. Constellations are 2-dimensional groupings of stars that may be different ages and degrees of brightness, and often are millions of light years apart.

7. Rockets and space travel have captured our imaginations, even if our ideas behind the physics aren't quite correct.

Who Are You ? And ...

First of all, we may have an emergency at hand and we'll both want to cut to the chase and get the patient into the cardiac unit if necessary. So, before we go too much further, **define yourself**. Please check one and only one choice listed below and then immediately follow the directions that follow *in italics*. Thank you in advance for your cooperation.

I am holding this book because …

   A. I am a responsible, but panicked, parent. My son / daughter / triplets (circle one) just informed me that his / her / their science fair project is due tomorrow. This is the only therapy I could afford on such short notice, which means that if I were not holding this book, my hands would be encircling the soon-to-be-worm-bait's neck.

Directions: Can't say this is the first or the last time we heard that one. Hang in there, we can do this.

1. Quickly read the Table of Contents with the worm bait. The Big Ideas define what each section is about. Obviously, the kid is not passionate about science, or you would not be in this situation. See if you can find an idea that causes some portion of an eyelid or facial muscle to twitch.

If that does not work, we recommend narrowing the list to the following labs because they are fast, use materials that can be acquired with limited notice, and their intrinsic level of interest is generally quite high.

Lab #4 • *Infrared Sponges* • *page 38*
Lab #13 • *Big Blue* • *page 63*
Lab #17 • *Jumpin' Jupiter Bolts* • *page 74*
Lab #25 • *Down in Front* • *page 98*
Lab #38 • *Homemade 'Scope* • *page 137*
Lab #44 • *Soup Can Constellation* • *page 155*
Lab #49 • *Sound Sponge* • *page 172*

How to Use This Book

2. Take the materials list from the lab write-up and from page 201 of the Science Fair Project section and go shopping.

3. Assemble the materials and perform the lab at least once. Gather as much data as you can.

4. Go to page 178 and read the material. Then start on Step 1 of Preparing Your Science Fair Project. With any luck, you can dodge an academic disaster.

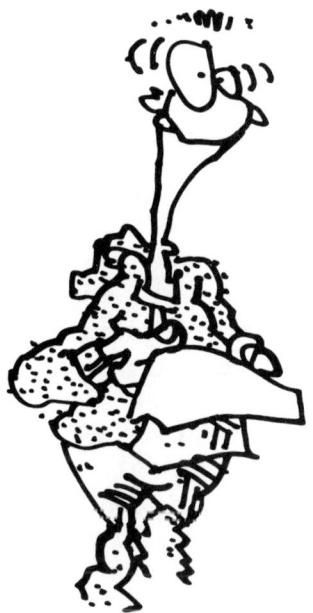

___ **B. I am worm bait.** My science fair project is due tomorrow, and there is not anything moldy in the fridge. I need a big Band-Aid, in a hurry.

Directions: Same as Option A. You can decide if and when you want to clue your folks in on your current dilemma.

___ **C. I am the parent of a student who informed me that he/ she has been assigned a science fair project due in six to eight weeks.** My son/daughter has expressed an interest in science books with humorous illustrations that attempt to explain astronomy and associated phenomena.

Who Are You ? And ...

Directions: Well, you came to the right place. Give your kid these directions and stand back.

1. The first step is to read through the Table of Contents and see if anything grabs your interest. Read through several experiments, see if the science teacher has any of the more difficult-to-acquire materials, like diffraction gratings, optical equipment, and some of the chemicals, and ask if they can be borrowed. Play with the experiments and see which one really tickles your fancy.

2. After you have found and conducted an experiment that you like, take a peek at the Science Fair Ideas and see if you would like to investigate one of those or create an idea of your own. The guidelines for those are listed in the Science Fair section. You have plenty of time, so you can fiddle and fool with the original experiment and its derivations several times. Work until you have an original question you want to answer and then start the process. You are well on your way to an excellent grade.

___ **D. I am a responsible student and have been assigned a science fair project due in six to eight weeks.** I am interested in astronomy, and despite demonstrating maturity and wisdom well beyond the scope of my peers, I too still have a sense of humor. Enlighten and entertain me.

Directions: Cool. Being teachers, we have heard reports of this kind of thing happening, but usually in an obscure and hard-to-locate town several states removed. Nonetheless, congratulations.

Same as Option C. You have plenty of time and should be able to score very well. We'll keep our eyes peeled when the Nobel Prizes are announced in a couple of decades.

How to Use This Book

___ **E. I am a parent who home schools my child/children.** We are always on the lookout for high-quality curriculum materials that are not only educationally sound but also kid- and teacher-friendly. I am not particularly strong in science, but I realize it is a very important topic. How is this book going to help me out?

Directions: In a lot of ways, we created this book specifically for home schoolers.

1. We have taken the National Content Standards, the guidelines that are used by all public and private schools nationwide to establish their curriculum base, and listed them in the Table of Contents. You now know where you stand with respect to the national standards.

2. We then break these standards down and list the major ideas that you should want your kid to know. We call these the Big Ideas. Some people call them objectives, others call them curriculum standards, educational benchmarks, or assessment norms. Same apple, different name. The bottom line is that when your child is done studying this unit on astronomy, you want them not only to understand and explain each of the Big Ideas listed in this book, but also to be able to defend and argue their position based on experiential evidence that they have collected.

3. Building on the Big Ideas, we have collected and rewritten 50 hands-on science labs. Each one has been specifically selected so that it supports the Big Idea that it is correlated to. This is critical. As the kids do the science experiment, they see, smell, touch, and hear the experiment. They will store that information in several places in their brains. When it comes time to comprehend the Big Idea, the concrete hands-on experiences provide the foundation for building the Idea, which is quite often abstract. Kids who merely read about radio galaxies, spectrum analysis, and distances between the planets, or who see pictures of quasars, supernovas, and constellations but have never tried to build one, are trying to build abstract ideas on abstract ideas and quite often miss the mark.

Who Are You ? And ...

*For example: I can show you a recipe in a book for chocolate chip cookies and ask you to reiterate it. Or I can turn you loose in a kitchen, have you mix the ingredients, grease the pan, plop the dough on the cookie sheet, slide everything into the oven, and wait impatiently until they pop out eight minutes later. Chances are that the description given by the person who actually made the cookies is going to be much clearer because it is based on their true understanding of the process, **because it is based on experience.***

4. Once you have completed the experiment, there are a number of extension ideas under the Science Fair Extensions that allow you to spend as much or as little time on the ideas as you deem necessary.

5. A word about humor. Science is not usually known for being funny even though Bill Nye, The Science Guy, *Beaker from* Sesame Street, *and* Beakman's World *do their best to mingle the two. That's all fine and dandy, but we want you to know that we incorporate humor because it is scientifically (and educationally) sound to do so. Plus it's really at the root of our personalities. Here's what we know:*

When we laugh ...
a. Our pupils dilate, increasing the amount of light entering the eye.
b. Our heart rate increases, which pumps more blood to the brain.
c. Oxygen-rich blood to the brain means the brain is able to collect, process, and store more information. Big I.E.: increased comprehension.
d. Laughter relaxes muscles, which can be involuntarily tense if a student is uncomfortable or fearful of an academic topic.
e. Laughter stimulates the immune system, which will ultimately translate into overall health and fewer kids who say they are sick of science.
f. Socially, it provides an acceptable pause in the academic routine, which then gives the student time to regroup and prepare to address some of the more difficult ideas with a renewed spirit. They can study longer and focus on ideas more efficiently.
g. Laughter releases chemicals in the brain that are associated with pleasure and joy.

6. If you follow the book in the order in which it is written, you will be able to build ideas and concepts in a logical and sequential pattern, but that is by no means necessary. For a complete set of guidelines on our ideas on how to teach home-schooled kids science, check out our book, Why's the Cat on Fire? How to Excel at Teaching Science to Your Home-Schooled Kids.

How to Use This Book

___ **F. I am a public/private school teacher,** and this looks like an interesting book to add ideas to my classroom lesson plans.

Directions: It is, and please feel free to do so. However, while this is a great classroom resource for kids, may we also recommend several other titles: EMS: It's Not What You Think *(Electromagnetic Spectrum),* Nine Neighbors and a Star *(The Solar System),* Seasons, Cycles, and Celestial Upstarts, *(Regular Astral Phenomena),* The Zodiac Cadillac *(Stars and Constellations),* and The Intergalactic Bus Pass *(Rockets, Probes, and Space Exploration).*

These books have teacher-preparation pages, student-response sheets or lab pages, lesson plans, bulletin board ideas, discovery center ideas, vocabulary sheets, unit pretests, unit exams, lab practical exams, and student grading sheets—basically everything you need if you are a science nincompoop, and a couple of cool ideas if you are a seasoned veteran with an established curriculum. All of the ideas that are covered in this one book are covered much more thoroughly in the other five. They were specifically written for teachers.

___ **G. My son/daughter/grandson/niece/father-in-law** is interested in science, and this looks like fun.

Directions: Congratulations on your selection. Add a gift certificate to the local science supply store and a package of hot chocolate mix and you have the perfect rainy Saturday afternoon gig.

___ **H. I watched Star Wars at least 600 times and the lasers and explosions were really, really loud every time. Are sure there is no sound in a vacuum?**

Directions: Yep. Check between your ears for verification.

Lab Safety

Contained herein are 50 science activities to help you better understand the nature and characteristics of astronomy as we currently understand these things. However, because you are on your own in this journey, we thought it prudent to share some basic wisdom and experience in the safety department.

Read the Instructions

An interesting concept, especially if you are a teenager. Take a minute before you jump in and get going to read all of the instructions as well as warnings. If you do not understand something, stop and ask an adult for help.

Clean Up All Messes

Keep your lab area clean. It will make it easier to put everything away at the end and may also prevent contamination and the subsequent germination of a species of mutant tomato bug larva. You will also find that chemicals perform with more predictability if they are not poisoned with foreign molecules.

Organize

Translation: Put it back where you get it. If you need any more clarification, there is an opening at the landfill for you.

HELLO.

GOODBYE.

Dispose of Poisons Properly

This will not be much of a problem with the labs that are suggested in this book. However, if you happen to wander over into one of the many disciplines that incorporates the use of more advanced chemicals, then we would suggest that you use great caution with the materials and definitely dispose of any and all poisons properly.

Practice Good Fire Safety

If there is a fire in the room, notify an adult immediately. If an adult is not in the room and the fire is manageable, smother the outbreak with a fire blanket or use a fire extinguisher. When the fire is contained, immediately send someone to find an adult. If, for any reason, you happen to catch on fire, **REMEMBER: Stop, Drop, and Roll.** Never run; it adds oxygen to the fire, making it burn faster, and it also scares the bat guano out of the neighbors when they see the neighbor kids running down the block doing an imitation of a campfire marshmallow without the stick.

Protect Your Skin

It is a good idea to always wear protective gloves whenever you are working with chemicals. Again, this particular book does not suggest or incorporate hazardous chemicals in its lab activities. However, if you do happen to spill a chemical on your skin, notify an adult immediately and then flush the area with water for 15 minutes. It's unlikely, but if irritation develops, have your parents or another responsible adult look at it. If it appears to be of concern, contact a physician. Take any information that you have about the chemical with you.

Lab Safety

Save Your Nose Hairs

Sounds like a cause celebre L.A. style, but it is really good advice. To smell a chemical to identify it, hold the open container six to ten inches down and away from your nose. Make a clockwise circular motion with your hand over the opening of the container, "wafting" some of the fumes toward your nose. This will allow you to safely smell some of the fumes without exposing yourself to a large dose of anything noxious. This technique may help prevent a nosebleed or your lungs from accidentally getting burned by chemicals.

Wear Goggles if Appropriate

If the lab asks you to heat or mix chemicals, be sure to wear protective eyewear. Also have an eyewash station or running water available. You never know when something is going to splatter, splash, or react unexpectedly. It is better to look like a nerd and be prepared than schedule a trip down to pick out a Seeing Eye dog. If you do happen to accidentally get chemicals in your eye, flush the area for 15 minutes. If any irritation or pain develops, immediately go see a doctor.

Lose the Comedy Routine

You should have plenty of time scheduled during your day to mess around, but science lab is not one of them. Horseplay breaks glassware, spills chemicals, and creates unnecessary messes—things that parents do not appreciate. Trust us on this one.

No Eating

Do not eat while performing a lab. Putting your food in the lab area contaminates your food and the experiment. This makes for bad science and worse indigestion. Avoid poisoning yourself and goobering up your labware by observing this rule.

Happy and safe experimenting!

Galactic Cookie Dough • B. K. Hixson

Recommended Materials Suppliers

For every lesson in this book, we offer a list of materials. Many of these are very easy to acquire, and if you do not have them in your home already, you will be able to find them at the local grocery or hardware store. For more difficult-to-acquire items, we have selected, for your convenience, a small but respectable list of suppliers who will meet your needs in a timely and economical manner. Call for a catalog or quote on the item that you are looking for, and they will be happy to give you a hand.

Loose in the Lab
9462 South 560 West
Sandy, UT 84070
Phone 1-888-403-1189
Fax 1-801-568-9586
www.looseinthelab.com

Nasco
901 Jonesville Avenue
Fort Atkinson, WI 53538
Phone 1-414-563-2446
Fax 1-920-563-8296
www.nascofa.com

Educational Innovations
151 River Road
Cos Cob, CT 06807
Phone 1-888-912-7474
Fax 1-203-629-2739
www.teachersource.com

Fisher Scientific
485 S. Frontage Road
Burr Ridge, IL 60521
Phone 1-800-955-1177
Fax 1-800-955-0740
www.fisheredu.com

Delta Education
80 NW Boulevard
Nashua, NH 03063
Phone 1-800-442-5444
Fax 1-800-282-9560
www.delta-education.com

Ward's Scientific
5100 W Henrietta Road
Rochester, NY 14692
Phone 1-800-387-7822
Fax 1-716-334-6174
www.wardsci.com

Frey Scientific
100 Paragon Parkway
Mansfield, OH 44903
Phone 1-800-225-FREY
Fax 1-419-589-1546
www.freyscientific.com

Sargent Welch Scientific Co.
911 Commerce Court
Buffalo Grove, IL
Phone 1-800-727-4368
Fax 1-800-676-2540
www.sargentwelch.com

The Ideas,
Lab Activities,
& Science Fair
Extensions

Big Idea 1

The sun is a medium-sized star at the center of our solar system. It radiates a spectrum of electromagnetic energy out into the universe.

Introducing the EMS

The Experiment

There are all kinds of waves out there: X-rays, gamma rays, cosmic rays, ultraviolet rays, radio waves, television waves, and the colors we see, called visible light rays. If you could see these waves, they would look like a series of sideways Ss that are all connected together. We are going to cover the very basics in this lab, starting with the name of this whole family of waves. Collectively they are called the electromagnetic spectrum, or EMS, and all stars produce and emit the following waves in order of length: gamma, X-rays, ultraviolet, visible light, infrared, microwaves, and radio waves, which are the longest.

Of all of these waves, the only ones that typically reach the surface of the Earth are the visible light, some ultraviolet, infrared, and a smattering of radio waves. Everything else is blocked out by the atmosphere.

Scientists measure different kinds of waves and classify the waves according to their measurements. But before we get into the measuring of waves, we need to give the different parts names. A complete wave is pictured at the right. The top of the wave is called the *crest* and the bottom of the wave is the *trough*. One complete cycle, up and down, is considered a *wave*.

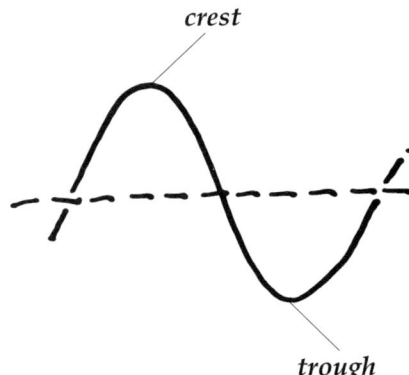

1 wave

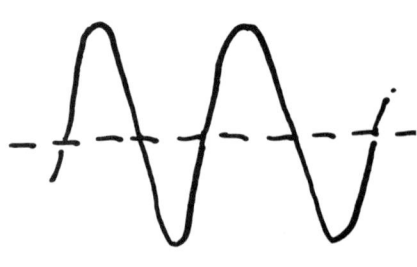

2 waves
higher frequency

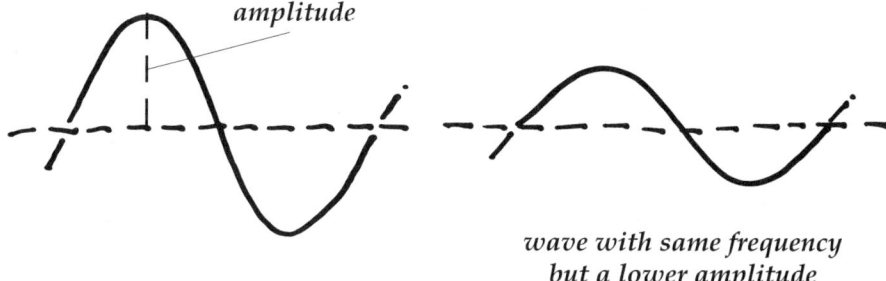

amplitude

wave with same frequency but a lower amplitude

The waves are measured two ways. First, one complete sideways S is measured. This is called the *frequency*. Take a centimeter. If one wave (a complete sideways S) fits perfectly in that distance, the frequency of that wave is measured at one wave per centimeter, or 1 centimeter. If two waves fit in the same distance, the frequency is now .5 centimeter. The higher the frequency, the tighter the Ss are packed together, and the more waves you can squish into a space.

The other measurement that is important is the *amplitude*. The amplitude is how high the S stretches up and down. For music waves, the amplitude is directly correlated to loudness. You can blow the same note into a trumpet over and over, and it will always vibrate at the same frequency. If you blow hard and produce a loud tone, it changes the amplitude but not the frequency. If you blow softly, the amplitude is smaller, but the frequency is exactly the same.

This lab is going to allow you to compare each of the waves present in the electromagnetic spectrum. You will stretch them out and compare the amount of energy that each one carries with it as it travels through space.

Materials

1   Pair of scissors
1   Meterstick
1   1.2-meter long strip of butcher paper
1   Wave descriptions

Introducing the EMS

Procedure

1. First things first. Before we build a model of the electromagnetic spectrum, you need to know the characteristics of the different forms of electromagnetic radiation that is pelting the Earth and its atmosphere. Starting from the shortest …

A. *Gamma rays* — We are going to start with the waves with the shortest frequencies, anything less than .01 nanometer (1 one-billionth of a meter). These waves have the most energy, and are produced by gamma ray bursters, which are super-powerful exploding stars.

B. *X-rays* — These waves are emitted by hot gasses that are between 1 million and 100 million degrees Celsius. Gases of these temperatures are found at the edges of galaxies and near black holes. X-rays from space do not make it to Earth. Instead, they are absorbed in the upper atmosphere.

C. *Ultraviolet rays* — The hottest stars emit most of their energy at these wavelengths. We are protected, in large part, from these rays by the ozone layer over the Earth, which reflects the majority of the energy. However, enough still gets through to create problems for many people who are not protected from these rays that are also responsible for weathering fabric, discoloring cars, and degrading plastics that are constantly being bombarded by them.

D. *Optical light waves* — This is the narrowest band of waves in the entire spectrum. Visible light waves have frequencies of between 390 and 700 mm, and in that narrow band of light, all of the colors of the rainbow are produced.

E. *Infrared waves* — Also known as heat radiation, these waves come from objects with temperatures of around 1000° C. These waves are generally absorbed in the lower atmosphere. Dark cloud-forming stars produce lots of infrared radiation.

F. *Radio waves*—These waves are emitted by many objects, from radio galaxies and remnants of supernovas to the leftovers from the Big Bang. Radio wavelengths of less than 100 meters are allowed to penetrate the Earth's atmosphere. All others are reflected back into space.

2. Now that the formalities are out of the way, you are going to construct a scale model so that you can see the relative proportions of each of the wavelengths in the electromagnetic spectrum. The scale that you are going to create is a general approximation, based on powers of 10.

3. You should have a whole sheet of butcher paper to work with. Start at the left side and write the word *wavelength* at the bottom of the page. Draw a one-meter long line across the bottom of the page, about one inch from the bottom. Start at 0 centimeters and mark the line every 5 cm with a pencil.

4. Starting with 0 cm, label each mark in order: 0.000.01 nm, 0.000.1 nm, 0.001 nm, .01 nm, .1 nm, 1 nm, 10 nm, 100 nm, 0.001 mm, 0.01 mm, 0.1 mm, 1 mm, 1 cm, 10 cm, 1 m, 10 m, 100 m, 1 km, and 10 km.

Introducing the EMS

5. Above the word *wavelength* on the lefthand side of the sheet of butcher paper, write the word *wave name*. Then, using the information in the *Data & Observations* section below, measure and mark the appropriate section of the meterstick with the corresponding wave's length. For example, starting at the lefthand side, measure from 0 cm to 25 cm, make a long, flat rectangular block, and write *Gamma Rays* inside it. Do the same for the other 5 wavelengths.

6. By now, you should have used the bottom five inches, at most, of the butcher paper. In the space above the *wave name*, leave one foot and find pictures of the instruments that detect and record the waves in the second data table in the *Data & Observations* section. Draw pictures of those instruments and find out what they have discovered.

7. Finally, in the top third of the butcher paper, research each of the Astrobodies listed in the second data table and draw pictures of what they look like above the kinds of waves they produce.

Data & Observations

Wave	Wavelengths	Measurement
Gamma	.01 nm or less	0 cm to 25 cm
X-rays	.01 nm to 10 nm	25 cm to 40 cm
Ultraviolet	10 nm to 390 nm	40 cm to 50 cm
Optical	390 nm to 700 nm	50 cm to 51 cm
Infrared	700 nm to 1 mm	51 cm to 65 cm
Radio	1 mm to 1 km	65 cm to 100 cm

Galactic Cookie Dough • B. K. Hixson

Wave	Instrument	Astrobody
Gamma	Compton Observatory Balloons	Quasars
X-rays	ROSAT Balloons	Cluster Galaxies
Ultraviolet	SkyLab Astrotelescope (Shuttle)	Sun's Corona
Optical	Hubble Telescope Telescopes	Stars, Galaxies, Etc.
Infrared	Infrared Observatory SOFIA	Various Stars
Radio	COBE Very Large Array Arecibo Observatory	Supernova Radio Galaxies

How Come, Huh?

This lab will give you a brief introduction to the electromagnetic spectrum, how we know that it exists, and the kinds of astronomical bodies that have been discovered. Needless to say, you are just getting started.

Science Fair Extensions

1. We are in the Golden Age of astronomy. You do not have to look very far back in the history books to find out who discovered what, and when they did it. Pick a wavelength and research the history and the science behind that branch of electromagnetic astronomy.

Spectrally Speaking

The Experiment

The visible light spectrum is a very, very small portion of the entire electromagnetic spectrum, but it provides us with all kinds of valuable information about the age of stars, how fast they are moving, and their relative temperature.

To collect this information about stars like our sun, astronomers use an instrument called a spectroscope.

Materials

1   Pair of diffraction grating glasses
3   Sources of white light (NEVER USE THE SUN!)
    1   Fluorescent bulb
    1   Incandescent bulb
    1   Candle flame
1   Commercial spectroscope
1   Set of colored pencils
Adult Supervision

Procedure

1. Put on the diffraction glasses and take a look at the fluorescent lights that are in the room. You should see a complete set of the colors of the rainbow. Record them in the correct order, in the spaces on the next page, starting with red. Draw a picture of the rainbow as it appears around the light.

a. _____ *red* _____

b. _____

c. _____

d. _____

e. _____

f. _____

g. _____

fluorescent light through diffraction grating

fluorescent light through a spectroscope

2. Now observe the same light using the commercial spectroscope. Record your observations in the drawing space above.

3. Repeat steps 1 and 2, using the diffraction grating and the spectroscope to observe an incandescent bulb. Then, with the supervision of an adult, observe a candle flame. Record your observations as drawings in the spaces provided on the next page.

Spectrally Speaking

incandescent light through diffraction grating

incandescent light through a spectroscope

candlelight through diffraction grating

candlelight through a spectroscope

How Come, Huh?

Diffraction grating is a special plastic film material that does the equivalent of what a prism can do: It splits the light you are viewing into its spectrum, or special color pattern, created by the elements that emit it. Different elements produce different and very unique color patterns that are seen when viewed through the spectroscope. These color patterns are unique to each element and can be used to identify the element much the same way that fingerprints can be used to identify people.

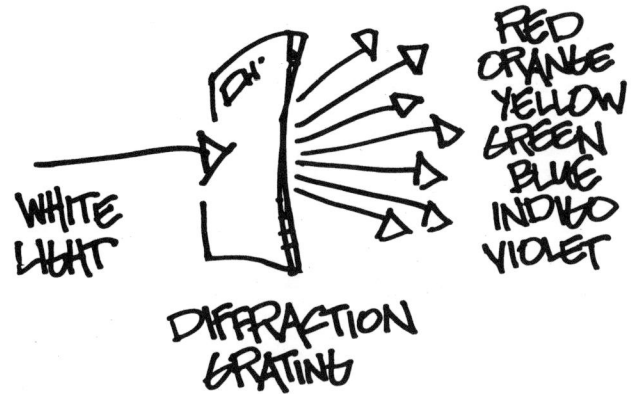

WHITE LIGHT

DIFFRACTION GRATING

RED
ORANGE
YELLOW
GREEN
BLUE
INDIGO
VIOLET

As light travels through the diffraction grating, the different wavelengths "bend" and separate into the same sequence as the colors of the rainbow. The difference in the size of the wavelengths is what produces the different colors. The shorter ones are the blues and violets. The longer ones are the reds and oranges.

When you look through a spectroscope, you will find that the color print consists of separate lines rather than large, wide bands like you see when a rainbow appears after a storm. The number and location of the color bands—red, orange, yellow, green, blue, and so on—are unique and are found only with that one element or compound.

Spectrally Speaking

Science Fair Extensions

2. There are sealed tubes of gas that can be electrified to excite the electrons. When these tubes are plugged in and viewed through a spectroscope, they produce specific color patterns. Create a display where these tubes of gas can be viewed, and compare the tubes with samples that have been burned in a flame.

3. Astronomers use finely tuned diffraction gratings to filter starlight that is collected through telescopes. This light can tell the astronomers what age a star is, its composition, and how fast it is moving away from the Earth. Collect information and build a spectro-photometer that can be used to view starlight.

4. Forensic labs that investigate crimes use spectroscopes to identify substances that are collected at the scene of the crime. Visit one of these labs and glean what information and technical data you can. Use it to construct your own instrument.

Sun's Up!

The Experiment

This particular lab demonstrates that visible light and infrared energy, both part of the electromagnetic spectrum produced by the sun, can be absorbed by a vane trapped in a glass bulb. The vane then releases the trapped energy, and that causes the vane to spin.

If you are following these ideas closely, you will recognize that you are going to use light and heat energy to produce motion. The previous labs introduced you to the idea of an entire electromagnetic spectrum, and then we peeled off the visible light portion of that spectrum.

Materials

1   Radiometer
1   Dark closet
1   Sunny day
1   Lamp
1   Table
1   Tall glass cylinder
    Water

Procedure

1. Place the radiometer on a level surface in a dark closet or cupboard where there is *little or no* sunlight. Look at the vanes inside the radiometer and estimate how fast they are spinning. Record your observation in the *Data* section on page 35. Place your hand in front of the bulb and record how much heat you felt. Record this information in the data table on page 36.

Sun's Up!

2. Place the radiometer on a level surface that has some *indirect sunlight,* and estimate and record the speed of the vanes. Place your hand in front of the bulb and record how much heat you felt. Record this information in the appropriate data table.

3. Place the radiometer on a level surface in *bright sunlight.* Estimate how fast the vanes are spinning. Record your observation. Place your hand between the sun and the radiometer and estimate the amount of heat you felt striking the radiometer. Record this information on page 36.

4. Place a bright lamp on a table and hold the radiometer near the lamp. Observe and record the speed at which the vanes are spinning when the radiometer is directly exposed to light from a lamp. Place your hand between the lamp and the radiometer and estimate the amount of heat you felt.

LAMP   VASE   RADIOMETER
              w/WATER

5. Now, place a tall cylinder (vase) of water between the lamp and the radiometer so that all the light striking the radiometer must pass through the cylinder of water first. Use the illustration on the previous page as a guide. (Vases work well as cylinders; those spaghetti holders you get at cooking stores work OK, too.) Record the speed at which the vanes spin using this setup. One last time, place your hand between the cylinder of water and the radiometer and estimate the amount of heat you felt.

Data & Observations

As you complete each step, put a check mark in the column that best describes the speed at which the vanes inside the radiometer were spinning.

Amount of Direct Light

Instruction	No Motion	Moderate	Fast	Very Fast
1				
2				
3				
4				
5				

Sun's Up!

Amount of Detectable Heat

Instruction	None	Some	Burnin', Baby
1			
2			
3			
4			
5			

How Come, Huh?

Radiometers can be used to detect two kinds of electromagnetic radiation (energy)—visible light that we see and infrared light that we feel as heat.

When infrared light strikes the vanes inside the radiometer, it reflects off the silvered side of the vane. But, when it strikes the black side, it is absorbed and converted to heat energy. This heat then escapes from the black side of the vane, expanding the air inside the radiometer and causing a small push against the black side of the vane. Bombard the radiometer with infrared light, and the vane spins pretty fast.

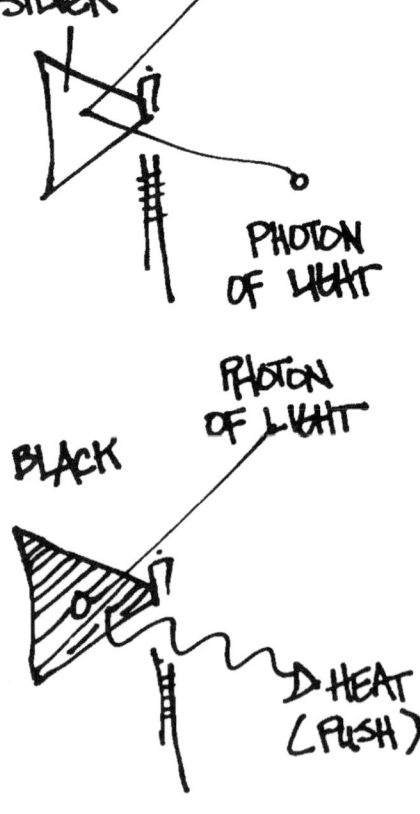

SILVER

PHOTON OF LIGHT

PHOTON OF LIGHT

BLACK

HEAT (PUSH)

The heat part of this experiment comes out in instructions 4 and 5. Lamps produce infrared heat waves. To know this, all you have to do is put your hand near a bulb. Water is very good about filtering out (absorbing) heat waves when light passes through it. By placing a cylinder of water between the lamp and the radiometer, you should have noticed a significant decrease in the speed of the vanes.

Science Fair Extensions

5. See if other liquids absorb infrared light. Try cooking oil, vinegar, rubbing alcohol, and anything else your parents give the thumbs-up to.

6. Locate other sources of infrared light (an electric stove comes to mind) and see if the radiometer can detect those waves—after you get your parents' permission, of course—using both the radiometer and the spectroscope from the experiment you just completed.

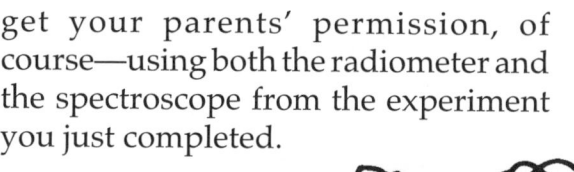

Infrared Sponges

The Experiment

This experiment is a great excuse to spend the day outside, catch some sunbeams in various colors of paper pockets, and record the ensuing temperature changes.

The sun produces all kinds of electromagnetic waves that are grouped as radiant energy, including visible light and infrared (heat) waves. Different colors react differently to this radiant energy: Some reflect it, others absorb it, and still others do a combination of things. This lab will examine how radiant energy and different colored objects interact with one another.

Materials

- 5 Thermometers
- 5 Sheets of paper
  - White
  - Red
  - Blue
  - Green
  - Black
- 1 Stapler
- 1 Clock

Procedure

1. Prepare 5 pockets using the colors of paper listed in the *Materials* section above. Fold each piece of construction paper hot-dog length (long and narrow, for you non-elementary types). Staple the bottom and side of each, to form a pocket.

HOT DOG FOLD

2. Put the thermometers into the pockets and take them out into the sun. Measure the temperature and start the clock running. Record the temperature of each pocket every minute for 10 minutes in the data table on the next page.

Data & Observations

Heating Colored Pockets

Time (mins.)	0	1	2	3	4	5	6	7	8	9	10
White											
Red											
Blue											
Green											
Black											

How Come, Huh?

White surfaces reflect white light and, as such, do not increase in temperature very much. Black surfaces absorb radiant light as well as the infrared light that accompanies it on its journey from the sun. The other colors fit in between the black and white.

Science Fair Extensions

7. Rather than using colored pockets, head to the wrapping store and purchase metallic-coated papers of different hues. Try silver, copper, and gold. Any difference?

8. Try water that has been dyed to produced different colors. Does black water absorb more radiant energy than red, green, or yellow water?

Concentrating Quanta

The Experiment

We saved this experiment for near the end of the infrared labs because it is probably the granddaddy of all light experiments and has been performed by almost every kid who ever held a hand lens. Light from the sun will be collected and concentrated using the lens. The effect of the concentrated light will allow you to solve the puzzle. (The term *quanta* is used to describe units or bundles of light energy.)

Materials

1   Quart jar, glass, with metal lid
1   Hammer
1   Nail, #6
1   Thread, 12 inches long
1   Paperclip
1   Hand lens, 3 to 5 inches in diameter
1   Sun

Procedure

1. Remove the metal lid from the jar and punch a hole in the center of it using the hammer and nail.

2. Feed the thread through the hole. Tie the paperclip to the end that will be outside the jar and the nail to the other end.

3. Lower the nail into the jar and screw the lid on. You will want to wind the thread around the paperclip so that the nail is dangling an inch or so above the bottom of the jar.

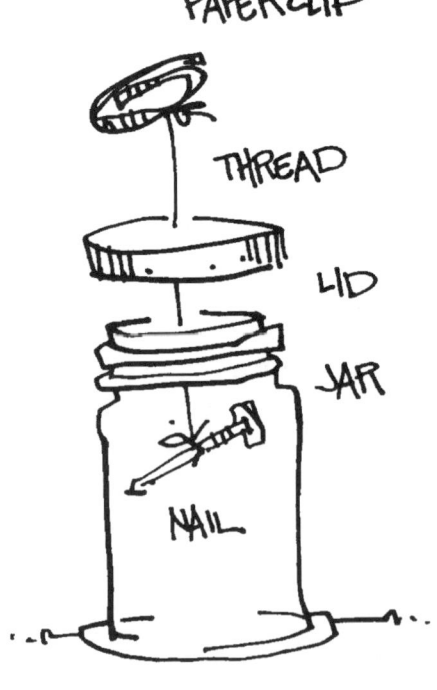

PAPERCLIP

THREAD

LID

JAR

NAIL

4. So, here is the puzzle: Without removing the lid or breaking the jar, figure out a way to "cut" the thread and get the nail to drop to the bottom of the jar. There is a fairly substantial clue in the illustration above.

How Come, Huh?

By focusing the light on the thread, the light energy gets concentrated on one point. As the energy accumulates in this one spot, the temperature of the thread increases until it reaches its kindling point, ignites, and burns. The nail falls to the bottom of the jar because it has gravity pulling on it.

Science Fair Extensions

9. Repeat the experiment using several different kinds of materials to hang the nail: thicker thread, string, fishing line, thin metal wire, human hair, and yarn, for starters. Measure the amount of time it takes for the material to ignite and burn.

10. Build and demonstrate a solar oven. As you do the research, you will find that it operates on the same basic principle of gathering and focusing light energy as your hand lens does.

UV Bead Converters

The Experiment

This is another photochemical response to sunlight, demonstrating the electromagnetic energy that is present in sunlight. The beads that you are going to use were produced using a chemical that is sensitive to ultraviolet sunlight. When the beads absorb the energy from this band of the electromagnetic spectrum, they convert the invisible light energy to visible light bands—colorful, fun, and some would even say magical.

The first part of this activity is simply to observe a color change that occurs when the beads absorb ultraviolet light and then radiate visible light. The lab suggests testing the effects of using a sunblock on the beads.

Materials

5   Ultraviolet beads
1   Pipe cleaner
1   Egg carton
1   Piece of clear, plastic wrap
1   Roll of masking tape
1   Pair of scissors
1   Bottle of sunblock (optional)
1   Sun

Procedure

1. String the five beads on the pipe cleaner and record the color of each bead beside the numbers 1 to 5 in the spaces provided on the next page.

2. Now, wear the pipe cleaner on your wrist, ankle, toe, or ear, and quietly go outside into the bright sunshine, taking this book and a pencil with you. Record your observations in the data table on the next page.

3. Prepare your egg carton by cutting a two-egg section from the bottom half of the tray. Take the beads off of the pipe cleaner and place two or three beads in each section of your egg carton. Put a piece of clear plastic wrap over one egg section and leave the other open.

4. Head outside once again and expose your beads to the sun. Record your observations below.

5. At this time, and with the permission of your folks, you may want to continue exploring light-blocking abilities by using fabrics, colored paper, different strengths of sunblock, or sunglass lenses.

Data & Observations

Bead #	Color Indoors	Color Outdoors
1		
2		
3		
4		
5		

Bead #	Uncovered	Covered in Plastic
1		
2		
3		
4		
5		

UV Bead Converters

How Come, Huh?

Ultraviolet waves are produced by all stars, including our sun. This light is transmitted through electromagnetic waves, or measurable waves, usually 0.28 microns to 0.40 microns. The longer waves are generally attributed to causing the production of melanin and a nice tan; the shorter ones rip right through the cells and cream the nuclei. We call that cancer if it gets out of hand.

The ultraviolet beads used in this experiment contain a pigment that absorbs the ultraviolet light from the sun and then radiates it back to us as visible light. The way we think this happens is described here:

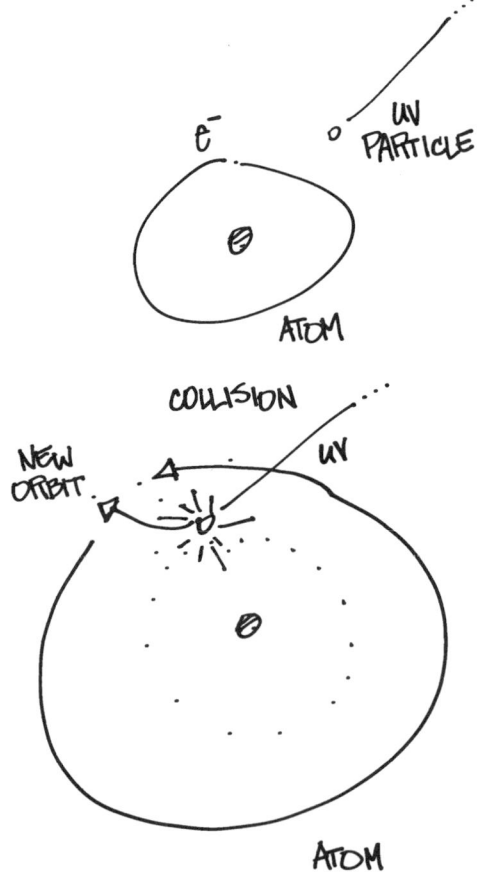

1. A photon of UV light zips away from the sun, travels 92,000,000 miles in about eight minutes, and zips through our atmosphere, dodging numerous obstacles to smash into the pigment, which happens to be a molecule, embedded in the bead. You have just added energy to the molecule, so something has to change. In this case …

2. The collision bumps one of the electrons (illustrated as *e*-) in the molecule from its regular, comfortable orbit to one that is a little bit farther away from the center of the atom. Translation: The energy from the light was absorbed by and stored in the electron's orbit, until …

3. This created an unstable situation and the electron, wanting to get rid of this extra energy, emits it as light that we see. It then returns to its regular orbit, where it continues to hover comfortably around the nucleus ... until the next UV particle creams the electrons again, bumping an unsuspecting electron into a new orbit ... and so it goes.

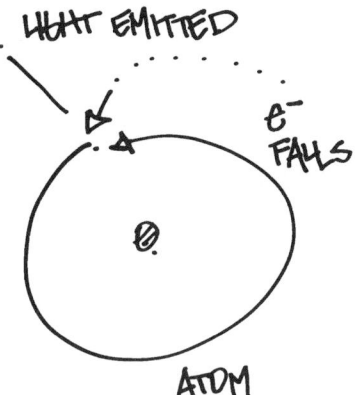

Science Fair Extensions

11.   Experiment with different sources of UV light. In addition to the sun, try tanning beds, food-heating lamps, various lightbulbs, and UV lamps. Rate the amount of color change and determine how juiced each of these sources is.

12.   Repeat the experiment using different brands of sunglasses. Check the glasses that are for sale in the store. Many of them claim that they block harmful UV rays. Place the UV beads in egg cartons and place a sunglass lens over each bead. Record the amount of the color change for each lens, and rate each on its effectiveness.

13.   Place the beads in the egg carton again and, this time, cover them with different materials, such as black fabric, cellophane, wax paper, aluminum foil, and anything else you can think of that might potentially block the UV rays. Record the color changes for each material.

14.   The company that manufactures these beads also produces UV-sensitive nail polish that changes colors in the sunlight. Design an experiment that uses that nail polish.

Sun-Powered Cells

The Experiment

So far, we have seen light cause a color change in paper and create a rainbow of colors in beads that contain special pigment. This lab will demonstrate that energy from either sunlight or artificial light can be captured and converted to electrical energy.

Materials

1   Solar cell
1   Simple motor
1   Fan attachment
2   Wires
1   Lamp (brighter is better)
1   Sun

Procedure

1. Commercial kits that contain all of the materials mentioned in the *Materials* section of this lab are readily available or, if you are a do-it-yourself kind of person, everything can be collected or purchased individually from your local hardware and hobby shop.

2. Identify the solar cell. It is usually a flat, black rectangle, with a clear, plastic top. Coming off the cell should be two wires, or connecting points. This is where you will collect the electricity produced by the cell and use it to run the motor.

SOLAR CELL

LEAD

MOTOR

3. Hook one wire to each connecting point on the solar cell. Then connect the wires to the two leads that come off the motor. You have just created a very simple series circuit. If you hold the solar cell in the sunshine or under a very bright lamp, the motor will begin to spin.

How Come, Huh?

Solar cells are made of a wafer of pure silicon, known as sand to most of us, that has been heated until it melts and then is poured into a thin rectangular shape and allowed to cool. When the silicon wafer was being poured, a small amount of the element, boron,

/ PHOTON
OF LIGHT

O ᴏ꒰Ꙩ O ꙨO ᴏ꒰ꙨꙨO N LAYER
ᴏ꒰ꙨO ꙨO ꙨO O O P LAYER

was added to the mix. This gives the wafer a positive electrical charge, so it is called a "P" (for positive) wafer.

Next, the engineers making these discs pour a very thin layer of pure silicon over the top of the "P" wafer. This mix contains a different additive, phosphorous, which gives the top half of the sandwich a negative charge. This is called the "N" wafer.

When a photon of light or particle of sunshine hits the solar cell, it bonks the electron from the top layer to the bottom one, producing a flow of electrons from the negative to the positive layers. Voila ... electricity from sunshine. What a country!

Science Fair Extensions

15. Different colors carry different amounts of energy with them, and when they strike the solar cells, that is reflected in the amount of energy that is gathered. Design an experiment and demonstrate that violet, blue, and green wavelengths of light contain more energy than red, orange, and yellow ones.

Gamma Ray Rocket

The Experiment

An Astroblaster is a physics toy that demonstrates all kinds of ideas. First, it demonstrates the idea of conservation of momentum, something that we will let a physics book explain. It can be used as a model to explain how and why some of the fastest moving particles in the universe, gamma rays, are emitted from stars. It also demonstrates Newton's Law of Action and Reaction, as well as force equals mass times acceleration.

Beyond all that, it is a great way to wind up chasing a little red ball all over your classroom, house, or down the street, if you are silly enough to drop this off the roof of your garage, like we were.

Materials

1   Astroblaster
1   Hard surface

Procedure

1. Your Astroblaster should be comprised of four balls stacked on a stick—each ball getting progressively smaller as you go up the stick. Take the small red ball off the top of the Astroblaster and hold it waist high. Drop it on a hard surface and see how far it rebounds up into the air.

2. Place the ball back on the top of the pile. Hold the Astroblaster by the top of the stick at waist height and drop it directly to the ground. Observe what happens to the little ball on the top of the pile.

3. Repeat the experiment if you can find your ball.

How Come, Huh?

As the Astroblaster fell toward the ground, all four balls and the stick fell as a unit. When the biggest ball hit the ground first, it collided with the floor and started to rebound. It immediately collided with the next-largest ball, transferring all of its energy to it. The second ball hit the third ball, which immediately smacked into the smallest ball.

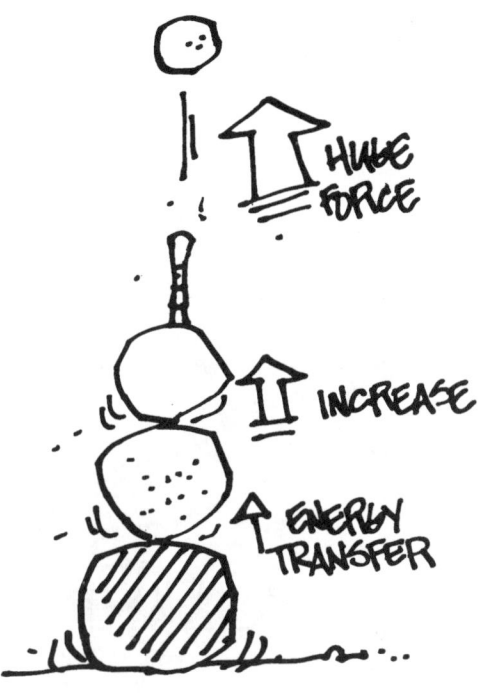

The upshot of all this whacking is that all the energy from the bottom three balls was transferred to the smallest ball. Using the famous conservation of momentum equation, $M_1V_1=M_2V_2$ where M stands for mass and V stands for velocity, the mass and velocity of the four balls dropped must equal the mass and velocity of just the small ball shooting up into the air. In order for this to be the case, the velocity must increase to make up for the loss of mass. The big ball is left behind. This is why the little ball takes off like it does.

Science Fair Extensions

16. On the packaging that comes with the commercial version of the Astroblaster, it claims that this is a model for supernovas. Do some research to find out why the inventors of this toy think that the little ball is like a gamma ray. Explain how in the world you could possibly simulate a supernova on your driveway.

Big Idea 2

In addition to the sun, our solar system is composed of nine planets that orbit our star.

Galactic Cookie Dough • B. K. Hixson

Micro Solar System

The Experiment

Any good astronomer will tell you that the solar system we live in is almost entirely space, even though we hardly ever think of it that way. In this lab, you will make a scale model of the solar system. You'll include all the planets, and then you'll position them at appropriate intervals to get a realistic idea of how far apart we are from our neighbors.

Materials

9   Tongue depressors
1   Playground ball, 9 inches in diameter
1   Sheet of paper
1   Pair of scissors
2   Metersticks
1   Metric ruler
1   Bottle of glue

Procedure

1. Label each of the 9 tongue depressors, one for each of the 9 planets. Use the data table on the next page for reference.

2. Using the data from the table, either draw or glue a circle measuring the appropriate diameter of the planet on each stick. For example, Mercury would be a very small circle, 1 mm in diameter. If the diameter of the planet exceeds the width of the tongue depressor, which is true for Saturn, make a paper model and glue it to the top of the stick.

Micro Solar System

Planet	Planet's Diameter (mm)	Distance from Sun (m)
Mercury	1	10
Venus	2	18
Earth	2	25
Mars	1	38
Jupiter	24	130
Saturn	20	238
Uranus	9	479
Neptune	8	750
Pluto*	1	1000

*Starting in 1980, a few astronomers questioned whether or not Pluto is a true planet. The debate ended in 1999, with Pluto officially holding onto its status as the ninth planet. As a result, the mnemonic phrase for remembering the planets—*My Very Educated Mother Just Served Us Nine Pizzas*—still applies.

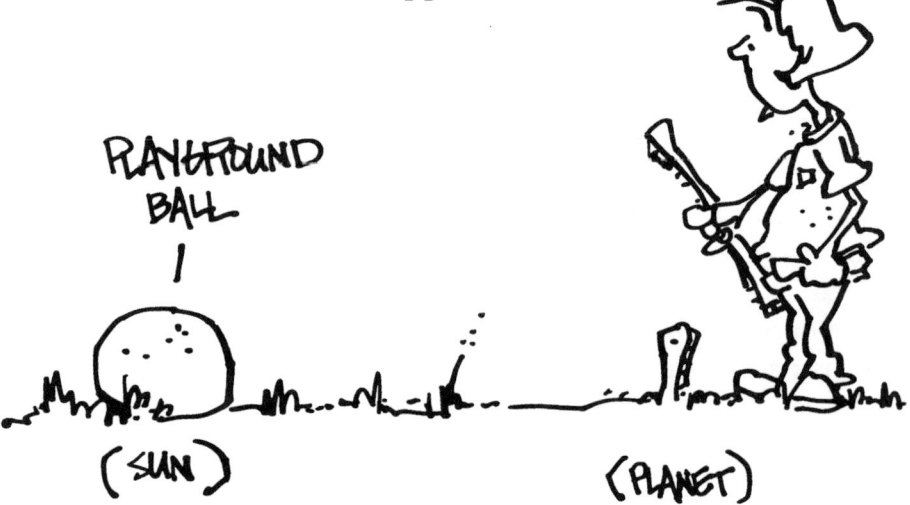

PLAYGROUND BALL

I

(SUN)

(PLANET)

Galactic Cookie Dough • *B. K. Hixson*

3. To build your solar system, place the playground ball at the far end of the playground. The ball will represent the sun at the correct scale size for our model. This will be your starting point.

4. Using the data from the table on the previous page, measure the distance from the sun to the first planet (Mercury) and push the tongue depressor representing Mercury into the grass. Repeat with the other planets. You'll notice that you are going to need a huge area to lay out all of the planets, considering the fact that Pluto is over 10 football fields from the sun. If it is not possible to spread things out perfectly, go as far as you can, or if your teacher gives you the green light, divide all of the distances by 10 so you can place the planets all within the space of a traditional football or soccer field.

How Come, Huh?

When you stand and look at this model, you can see that the four planets closest to the sun are actually stacked very close together with respect to the entire solar system. The outer gas planets are quite far away and the distances between them are very great.

Science Fair Extensions

17. Reduce the model even further and squish it down to the size of a meterstick. Assuming that Pluto is at the 100 cm mark, you can back all of the other planets out from there.

18. It is estimated that it would take a manned space flight five months to reach Mercury based on the data we have from the Mariner 10 program. Based on that information, calculate the travel time to the other planets in the solar system. Create a travel brochure extolling the virtues of the planets, try to entice others to come visit, and explain what you will do during the trip to get there and back.

Mercury's Hidden Face

The Experiment

First up is Mercury. The planet is very small and very close to the sun. In fact, a year on Mercury, or one revolution around the sun, takes only 88 days to complete. With the development of more and more powerful telescopes, it became easier and easier to view the surfaces of objects. However, the exception to this is Mercury.

This lab delves into the reason for this phenomenon. Mercury is so close to the sun that it is almost impossible to see its surface due to the intense light that is surrounding it, as you shall see.

Materials

1   Sheet of black construction paper
1   Sheet of newsprint
1   Soup can, empty, clean
1   Pair of scissors
1   Roll of masking tape
1   Craft stick
1   Meterstick
1   Light source
1   Darkened room

NEWSPRINT

↓

BLACK

CONSTRUCTION
PAPER

↓

CRAFT
STICK

Procedure

1. Tracing the soup can's end on the construction paper, cut a circle out of the paper and tape it to the top of the craft stick.

2. Do the same thing with a section of the local newspaper. Be sure to select a section where it is mostly print and not many pictures, illustrations, or cartoons.

3. Direct the light source so that it is shining directly into your eyes. Hold the newsprint side of the disc toward you and place it directly in front of the light. Use the illustration above as a guide. Then draw a picture of what you see in the box provided below. Try to read some of the text on the news page. Write down what you think it says in the space provided.

4. Move the disc to the right of the light source, keeping it very close and to the left of the light. Attempt to read the information on the newsprint side of the disc. Record what you read.

Data & Observations

directly in front of light

Mercury's Hidden Face

left of light

How Come, Huh?

The light is so intense that it interferes with your ability to see the surface of the disc and read the newsprint. The same is true of Mercury, when we try to look at it from Earth when the sun is in the background.

Science Fair Extensions

19. The U.S. sent a probe called Mariner 10 to Mercury. Find out the nature of the mission and see how successful it was in terms of taking photographic images of the surface of this planet.

20. Explain why your birthday would occur more often than sunrise if you lived on Mercury.

Atmospheric Opacity

The Experiment

Next up is Venus, which has a very thick, heavy atmosphere made up of carbon dioxide clouds that completely obscure the surface of the planet. Again, the appearance of the surface of the planet and how light interacts with it is an issue.

When light strikes an object, it can be completely reflected, absorbed, diffused, or transmitted. The terms used to describe these phenomena are *opaque, translucent,* and *transparent.* They are the focus of this lab, which will give you an idea of why it is so difficult to see the surface of Venus from Earth using a conventional telescope.

Materials

1   Sheet of wax paper
1   Sheet of clear plastic wrap
1   Pair of scissors
2   Rubberbands
2   Toilet paper tubes
1   Flashlight

COVERING

RUBBER-
BAND

TOILET PAPER
TUBE

Procedure

1. Cut each of the sheets of wax paper and clear plastic wrap in half.

2. Take one of the sheets of plastic wrap and wrap it around the end of one of the toilet paper tubes. Secure it with one of the rubberbands. Do the same thing with the other toilet paper tube and piece of plastic wrap, so that you have a matched set.

3. Hold the tubes up to your eyes and attempt to look around the room. Record your observations in the *Data* section on the next page.

Atmospheric Opacity

4. Repeat the procedure, making and using a set of wax paper binoculars. Record your observations below.

5. Set one of each tube—plastic wrap and wax paper—on a table about 5 feet away from you. Dim the lights so the room is as dark as you can get it, and shine a flashlight on the two surfaces attached to the toilet paper tubes.

6. Compare the amount of light that is reflected from the plastic wrap to the amount of light that is reflected from the wax paper.

Data & Observations

1. Type of image seen when looking around the room with:

      A. Plastic Wrap: _____

_____

      B. Wax Paper: _____

_____

2. Type of reflection seen when looking at the reflected surfaces of:

      A. Plastic Wrap: _____

_____

      B. Wax Paper: _____

_____

How Come, Huh?

The wax paper reflects some of the light that strikes it and allows some of it to pass through. This produces a fuzzy image that is described as *translucent*. This is why the planet Venus looks so bright in the night sky. The heavy, carbon dioxide clouds reflect most of the light from the sun back to Earth.

There have been a number of visits to Venus by U.S. space probes: Mariner 2, Venera 4, Venera 7, Mariner 10, Venera 9, Pioneer-Venus 2, and Magellan, to name a few. These visits have helped scientists discover that the atmosphere of Venus is 96% carbon dioxide, which creates surface temperatures of almost 900 degrees Fahrenheit and no moons. This has nothing to do with the atmosphere, but as we get farther and farther out, some of the planets have a whole pigpile of moons in orbit.

The clear plastic allows virtually all of the light to pass through, and is classified as *transparent*. When we look at Mercury, the Moon, or Mars, we can see right down to the surface of these bodies because their atmospheres are either extremely thin or nonexistent. There is nothing to block the view of the surface.

Science Fair Extensions

21. Create an experiment that demonstrates the differences in densities of a carbon dioxide atmosphere (Venus) vs. a nitrogen/oxygen atmosphere (Earth).

22. Venus has phases just like the Moon that orbits our Earth. Given that information, postulate what you believe the phases of Venus would look like, and create a model to show how things would look.

Greenhouse Atmosphere

The Experiment

Scientists have discovered that the atmosphere of Venus is 96% carbon dioxide, which creates surface temperatures of almost 900 degrees Fahrenheit. If that little tidbit of trivia simply slid in one ear and out the other, we would like to run it through the gauntlet again, with a little bit of neural Velcro this time. 900 degrees Fahrenheit. Why? That's the point of this lab.

Materials

2   Quart jars with lids
1   Sheet of wax paper
3   Thermometers
1   Clock with second hand
1   Sun or lamp

Procedure

1.   Find a nice sunny location or, if the weather is being uncooperative, find a high-powered lamp.

2.   Place one thermometer on a flat surface with sun(light) shining on it. Place a second thermometer inside one of the quart jars and put the lid on it.

3.   Line the third jar with wax paper, insert the thermometer, and put the lid on this jar. Then, line all three thermometers up.

4.   In the *Data & Observations* section, record the temperature readings of each of the three thermometers every five minutes for one hour and use that data to draw conclusions about why the atmospheres of the Earth and Venus are so different, and in particular, why the surface temperatures of both planets are so different.

Data & Observations

Time	Bare Thermometer	Clear Jar	Wax Jar
0			
5			
10			
15			
20			
25			
30			
35			
40			
45			
50			
55			
60			

Greenhouse Atmosphere

How Come, Huh?

When you look at the three temperatures, you are looking at models for Mercury (bare thermometer), which has almost no atmosphere, Venus (wax jar), which has a heavy, dense carbon dioxide atmosphere, and Earth (clear jar), which has an atmosphere, but one that is much thinner than that of Venus.

With the first model, there is nothing to prevent the heat from striking the surface of the planet and then radiating back into space. With Venus, the cloud layer over the planet is so thick and dense that any heat that penetrates that cloud layer bounces off the surface and then is reflected again by the cloud layer. This is why Venus is the hottest planet in the solar system.

Earth also has a cloud layer, but it is not thick and persistent. So, whereas heat is absorbed by the planet, much of it is re-radiated back into space. That is why clear, starry nights are so much colder than overcast nights. The cloud layer acts like a big blanket over the Earth.

Science Fair Extensions

23. Venus is only one of two planets with a backward rotation. (The other is Pluto.) Find out how this affects the length of the day, the atmosphere, and the speed at which the atmosphere travels over the surface of that planet.

Big Blue

The Experiment

There is the age-old question queried from youngster to parent, "Dad, why is the sky blue?" If you are in the majority, you will draw a blank until you get done with this lab. Once you're finished though, you'll even know why sunsets are red, orange, and yellow, but are rarely green or violet. (In case you were wondering, we've now migrated over to Earth.)

Materials

1   Large clear container (baking dish)
    Water
1   Flashlight
1   Index card
1   Container of powdered milk
1   Spoon

Procedure

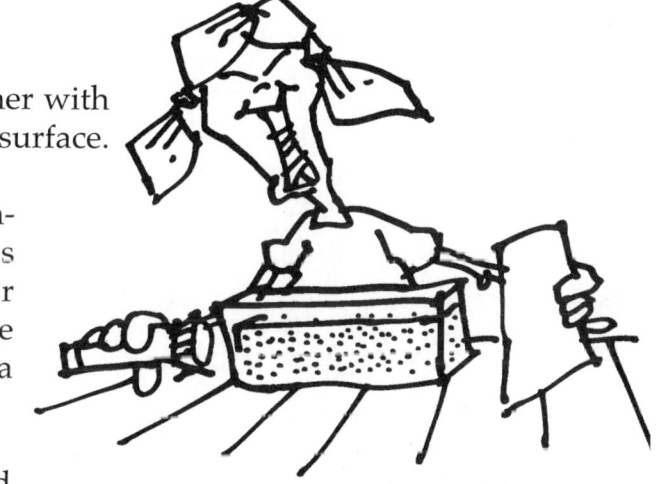

1. Fill the container with water and set it on a level surface.

2. Place the flashlight so that it shines through the container lengthwise and so that the beam can be reflected off a white index card.

3. Add powdered milk to the water, a pinch at a time, stirring with the spoon until you can see the beam as it shines through the liquid.

4. Look at the beam of light from the side of the container and at the end of the container. Record the colors that you see in the data table on the next page.

Big Blue

Data & Observations

Location	Color(s)
End	
Side	

How Come, Huh?

As the sunlight enters our atmosphere, it bounces off the gas molecules. The faster blue wavelengths of light tend to run into and be scattered by the gas molecules. The longer red and orange wavelengths tend to zip on by and go directly to the Earth. The same thing happens in the milky water. The blue wavelengths tend to bounce into the fat molecules and get scattered sideways, whereas the red-orange waves cruise on through to the end of the tank.

What this means for astronauts, astronomers, and aliens on vacation to the Earth, is that the Earth appears blue from space. This is because the shorter, faster blue and purple wavelengths are reflected off the atmosphere back into space, where they are detected by the viewer.

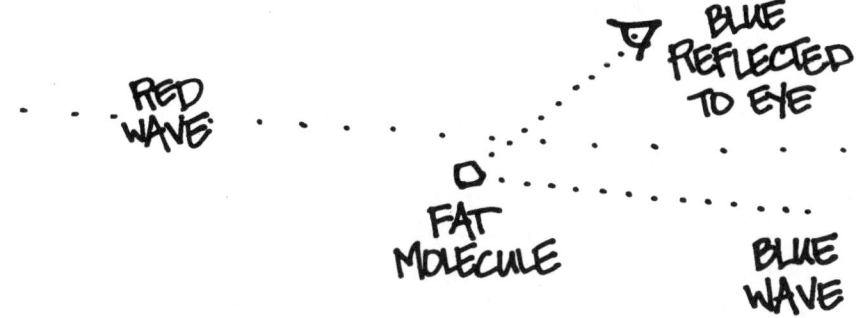

RED WAVE

BLUE REFLECTED TO EYE

FAT MOLECULE

BLUE WAVE

When you are on the ground, especially at daybreak or sunset, the longer red and orange wavelengths tend to bounce off the clouds in the atmosphere and produce beautiful effects. If you watch a sunset, it will actually progress through half the colors of the rainbow as the sun sets lower and lower in the sky. It will start out yellow, will move to orange, and then finally will turn deep-red before settling into darkness.

Science Fair Extensions

24. Experiment with the powder you add. Try cornstarch, talcum powder, chalk dust, and so forth.

25. Scattered light becomes polarized. Grab a polarizing filter, look at the end of the tank, and rotate the filter to notice the variance in the intensity of light.

Rusty Red Planet

The Experiment

Mars was named after the Roman God of War because it appears blood-red when you look at it through a telescope—probably what many battlefields looked like when the carnage was being assessed. The red color comes from a compound called iron oxide, which is present in great abundance in the many rocks that were produced by the volcanic activity of Mars.

To understand how iron is diffused in the lava to produce the basic black color that you see in all specimens, and also to understand the process that causes iron to oxidize and produce the red colors found in some specimens, we present today's lab for answers and enlightenment.

Materials

1   Steel wool pad
      (non-soap variety)
    Water
1   Tart pan
1   India ink
1   8-oz. glass
1   Sample of vocanic cinders

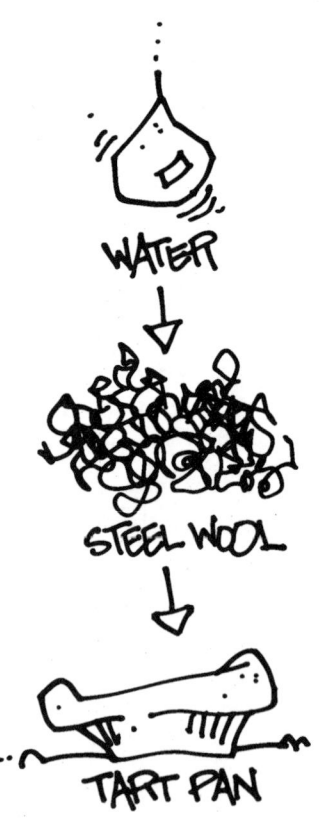

WATER

STEEL WOOL

TART PAN

Procedure

1. Fill the glass with water.

2. Place one drop of black India ink in the glass and observe how it diffuses through the water. You will see patterns start to form as the heavier ink flows toward the bottom of the glass. (The iron present in obsidian shows similar patterns.)

3. The steel wool should be the kind that is found in the paint section of a hardware store and that does not have any soap. (00000 grade is best.) Soak the piece of steel wool in a glass of water. Squeeze out the excess water and place it in the tart pan. Leave it overnight and observe the changes the next day.

How Come, Huh?

The water reacts with the iron in the presence of oxygen to produce iron oxide (rust). If your sample of cinders has rust-colored streaks, compare the color to the rust in the steel wool. You will see that the colors are about the same. As the lava cooled and solidified, some of the iron oxidized and colored the normally-black cinders.

When Mars is viewed with a telescope, the red color of the iron oxide dominates the view. This is why Mars is referred to as the "Red Planet."

Science Fair Extensions

26. Experiment using different temperatures of water. Compare the rates of diffusion as you place the same number of drops of ink in the glass.

27. Create artificial lava and then design an experiment to demonstrate how the red (oxidized iron) color could have been diffused through the magma as it flowed from the vent.

28. Repeat the second half of this experiment using the steel wool but, this time, place the wet steel wool inside a soda pop bottle, partially inflate a balloon, and insert the balloon over the opening of the bottle. Let the reaction stand for 24 hours and then observe what happened to the gas inside the balloon. Do a little research to learn why this reaction happened.

Olympus Mons(ter)

The Experiment

You have probably noticed that a lot of volcanic rocks have bubbles in them. The bubbles are the by-products of dissolved gas and water that boils once the lava erupts onto the surface of the Earth.

Sometimes the lava does not make it all the way out of the vent. The lava that coats the side of the vent is heated and then cools. It's then reheated with the next explosion, so it undergoes a lot of violent changes.

When you look at the surface of Mars, despite the fact that Mars is almost exactly the same size as Earth, the features are incredible. For example, there are many large canyons on Mars. The granddaddy of them all is called Valles Marineris. It is 2,800 miles long and 4 miles deep. To put this in perspective, the Grand Canyon of Arizona, the largest canyon on Earth, is 1 mile deep and stretches for about 250 miles. You could fit 40 Grand Canyons in one Valles Marineris.

Not only does Mars excel in holes, but it also has some pretty impressive volcanos. In fact, the largest mountain in the solar system, as far as we know, is a shield volcano on the surface of Mars, called Olympus Mons. It is a staggering 15.5 miles high. Mt. Everest, the tallest peak on Earth, is a measly 5.5 miles and change. This lab will give you an opportunity to recreate the kinds of lava flows that produce shield volcanos.

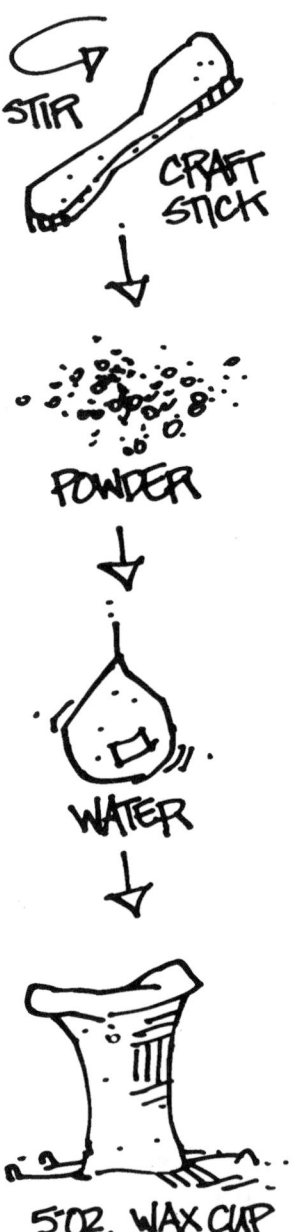

STIR

CRAFT STICK

POWDER

WATER

5 OZ. WAX CUP

Materials

1   7/8-oz. bottle of aluminum sulfate powder
1   7/8-oz. bottle of sodium bicarbonate powder
1   1-oz. bottle of liquid detergent
1   5-oz. wax cup
1   Craft stick
1   Toobe
1   Tart pan, 5 inches in diameter

Procedure

1. Add three ounces of water to the wax cup. Remove the cap from the bottle of aluminum sulfate powder. Fill the cap with powder and empty it into the wax cup.

2. Stir the powder until it has all dissolved. Then empty the contents of the wax cup into the Toobe.

3. Rinse the wax cup with water and repeat step 1 using the sodium bicarbonate powder. This time, add a dash of liquid detergent to the cup after you have stirred all of the powder into solution.

4. Place the Toobe in the center of the tart pan. Time for the "eruption." Slowly add the baking

BAKING SODA
SOLUTION

ALUMINUM
SULFATE
SOLUTION +
SOAP

TOOBE

Olympus Mons(ter)

soda solution to the aluminum sulfate. As the two chemicals react with each other, they will produce large quantities of carbon dioxide gas.

This gas will be trapped in the liquid because the detergent provides strength to the walls of the bubbles. As the number of gas bubbles increases, the bubbles run out of room near the surface of the liquid and start to push the bubbles that were formed at the bottom up and out of the Toobe.

5. If you examine the foam in the neck of the Toobe, you will see that it has lots of bubbles. You can also see that some of the bubbles burst or get damaged in the eruption. The same thing happens in a volcanic vent.

How Come, Huh?

This is similar to what happened in the volcanic vent on Mars that produced Olympus Mons and the other shield volcanos. Shield volcanos are typically large, flat mountainous regions that spread out over a very large area, the same way that pancake batter spreads out over a hot griddle.

The reaction between the two liquids produced a gas called carbon dioxide that expanded and oozed up and out of the Toobe. The gas bubbles got trapped in this liquid residue and produced a cavity, or hole, in the finished product. The soap gives the bubbles stability so that they can hang around longer.

Science Fair Extensions

29. Two of Mars' more interesting geological features are not actually on the surface of the planet but are in orbit around it. Mars has two moons, Deimos, which means "terror," and Phobos, which means, "fear." It seems to us that a simple "No Trespassing" sign would have been simpler. Find out how astronomers believe these two objects came to be moons of Mars, and what their identities were before each acquired the title of "moon."

30. Given the fact that there is a lot of volcanic activity present on the surface of the planet, make a list of rocks, landforms, and other features that you would look for if you were to land on Mars and begin exploring.

Jupiter Sun Prints

The Experiment

Off across the solar system to the gas giants! The next four planets in our studies are huge when compared with the inner four planets, have extreme climates and features, and continue to provide new information to astronomers.

Jupiter is the largest of the planets, and pictures of Jupiter reveal large bands of swirling colored clouds. Because the atmosphere of Jupiter is 90% hydrogen and 10% helium, both colorless gases, it has been postulated that the colored bands may be caused by a photochemical reaction between the trace elements in the clouds and sunlight—similar to this experiment.

Materials

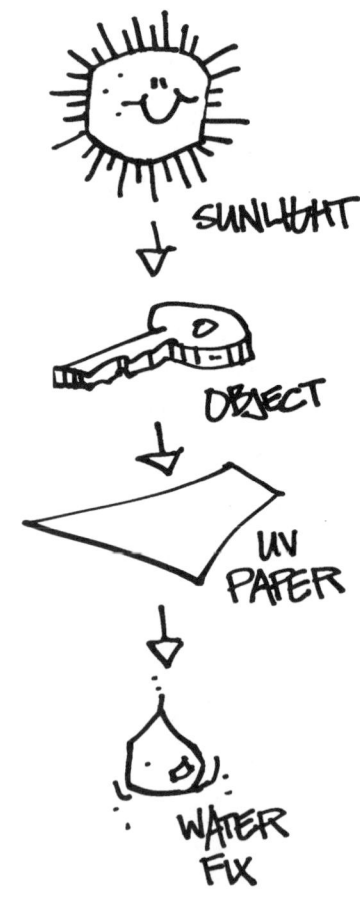

1 Sheet of light-sensitive paper
2 Small opaque objects
2 Small transluscent objects
1 Sun
1 Pencil
1 Large plastic tub
  Water

Procedure

1. Collect several opaque objects. These are things that light **cannot** pass through, like paperclips, keys, and pencils. Also find 2 or 3 items that are transluscent, like plastic, wax paper, etc.

2. Take the black envelope containing the light-sensitive paper and your objects outside into the sunshine.

3. Open the envelope and place the paper, blue-side up, in the sunshine. Place opaque objects you've collected on the light-sensitive paper and leave them in the bright sunshine until the paper turns a pale blue. It should take about two minutes, but if you are doing this lab on a cloudy day, it may take a bit longer. DO NOT OVEREXPOSE THE PAPER.

4. Remove the objects. Place the sheet of exposed paper in a tub of water for one minute. When time is up, take the sheet out of the water and place it on a flat surface to dry.

How Come, Huh?

The paper you are using is light sensitive. That means that if it is exposed to the sun, it will change color. Think about what it means to be opaque, translucent, and transparent. If you place an opaque object on the paper, the light will be blocked out, so the paper will not change color under that area. In areas where some or all of the light can reach the paper, a photochemical change takes place. It is believed that the same process occurs in the atmosphere of Saturn.

Science Fair Extensions

31.   Sunblocks are rated for their effectiveness at blocking ultraviolet rays. Acquire samples of sunblocks with various ratings: 0 (some of the tropical oils have no ability to block UV light), 2, 4, 6, 15, and 45. While you are inside a dimly lit room, write your name with each of the sunblocks on the light-sensitive paper. Be sure to identify each sample using a pen or pencil. Then, stick the paper outside and see how each sunblock does.

Jumpin' Jupiter Bolts

The Experiment

Probes sent to Jupiter have observed huge, superbolts of lightning in the atmosphere of the planet. It is believed that these bolts of lightning are created by the friction that is generated in the atmosphere by very fast-moving clouds. You, on the other hand, are going to incorporate some fast-moving rabbit fur.

To do this experiment, we are going to take advantage of the fact that fluorescent tubes are filled with gases that are easily excited by electricity and electrostatic charges. When they are exposed to electric charges, the electrons in the gases are attracted to the glass that has been coated with a compound called phosphor. When the electrons pass through the phosphor, they produce light.

Materials

1 Milk crate
    (or wooden chair)
1 Assistant
1 Dark room
1 Fluorescent lightbulb
1 Piece of rabbit fur

Procedure

1. Stand on the milk crate and ask your assistant to darken the room.

2. Hold the base of the fluorescent bulb with one hand and give the rabbit fur a good rub.

As you rub the fur on the bulb vigorously, look for sparks. Every now and then, lift the fur completely away from the bulb, look, and listen to what happens.

How Come, Huh?

The reason that you are standing on the milk crate is to insulate you from the Earth, which is a very good conductor. Doing this allows you to build up a larger, more dramatic charge.

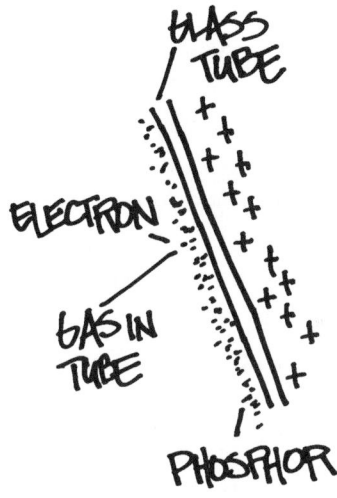

By rubbing the rabbit fur on the lightbulb, you are collecting electrons from the glass. This leaves the rabbit fur negatively charged and the surface of the glass bulb positively charged.

The positively charged surface of the glass attracts electrons from the gases trapped inside the bulb to the outside. To get there, they must pass through a coating on the inside of the fluorescent bulb. If you have ever broken a fluorescent bulb open, then you've seen this fine, whitish coating powder called phosphor.

As the electrons pass through the phosphor, they excite it, and this produces a visible glow that you can see. This glow can also be produced when electricity jumps from the negatively charged rabbit fur back to the positively charged glass bulb. When the discharge hits the bulb, it excites the phosphor, and the bulb glows again.

Science Fair Extensions

32. Find a Van de Graaff machine lying around the local high school physics lab. Plug it in, stand on the milkcrate, and pretend you are a probe descending into the clouds of Jupiter.

33. There are many materials that will create a static charge: plastic wrap, cellophane, nylon, and wool. Experiment and see if any one of these works better than the rabbit fur.

Seeing Saturn's Rings

The Experiment

You cannot see light unless you look directly at its source, or the light waves reflect off a surface to your eye. You will demonstrate this by shooting a single beam of light across a dark room. You won't be able to see the light until you reveal it, using talcum powder.

By the same token, Saturn, which is famous for its rings, is also a very large ball of hydrogen and helium. Surrounding the planet is a series of very large, flat rings. It is believed that the particles, ash and dust for the innermost rings, may have come from eruptions on Io, one of Saturn's 18 moons. This lab will give you an idea of how sunlight is intercepted by the dust in these rings so that they may become visible to the naked eye.

Materials

1   Index card
1   Hole punch
1   Flashlight
1   Roll of tape
1   Bottle of talcum powder
1   Dark room

CARD W/ HOLE

TAPE

Procedure

1. Using the hole punch, make a hole in the center of the index card.

2. Tape the index card to the front of the flashlight so that the bulb is lined up directly with the hole in the card.

3. Darken the room and turn the flashlight on. Shine the light around the room and try to see the beam—not the dot of light reflecting off the wall, chair, desk, or other object, but the actual beam. You can't.

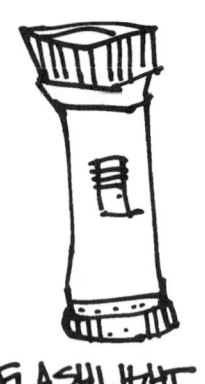

FLASHLIGHT

4. Holding the flashlight parallel to the ground or placing it on a tabletop to keep it steady, sprinkle a small amount of talcum powder where the beam of light appears to be shining. If your guess is correct, the beam will appear.

5. Let the beam settle for a minute, and then add more talcum powder. (If you have two erasers full of chalk dust, give them a bang and you will see the rings reappear.)

How Come, Huh?

Light cannot be seen unless it is viewed directly at the source or is reflected off a surface to your eyes. In this case, the beam zipped through the darkened room undetected until it hit the wall or some other object and was reflected to your eye. When you sprinkled talcum powder, the air was filled with little obstacles that reflected light to your eye. As the zillions of particles of light traveled through the beam, many of them collided with the talcum powder, and some were reflected to your eye.

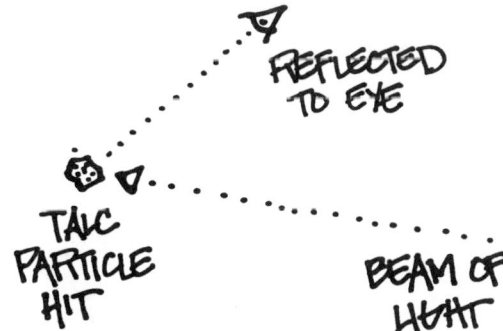

REFLECTED TO EYE

TALC PARTICLE HIT

BEAM OF LIGHT

Seeing Saturn's Rings

Science Fair Extensions

34.   Arrange a series of mirrors so they are lined up to bounce light from one to another. Turn the lights off and turn a flashlight on. The beams of light traveling between the mirrors will be invisible until you walk around the room sprinkling talcum powder to reveal the light beams. This technique is used in a lot of spy and thief movies to reveal laser security beams criss-crossing the floors of museums and high-tech factories.

35.   Figure out what other materials you can use to reveal a beam of light. Be sure to ask your mom before you start sprinkling baking soda and powdered sugar on the kitchen floor.

36. Saturn has more moons than any other planet in the solar system—18 and counting. Some of them, like Io, are believed to be contributing to the rings by dumping gas and dust from their volcanos. Plot each of the rings and moons, and decide how each came to be part of this huge planet.

Gas Giant #3

The Experiment

The seventh planet from the sun and the third of the four gas giants is Uranus, named for the Greek muse, Urania, who is also the patron goddess of astronomy. Uranus is different from all of the other planets in the solar system in that it is tipped on end. It has rings running from top to bottom instead of around its equator, and to make things more interesting, its magnetic field is off-center as well.

To attempt to explain these and other phenomena, there is a funny looking top, called a flipover top. It looks like a wooden apple with a really big stem. The question at hand today is, figure out if this top, which rotates down onto its stem as it spins, works if it spins clockwise *and* counterclockwise or works in only one direction. Try to figure out why this is the case and what this has to do with Uranus.

Materials

1   Flipover top
1   Hard surface
1   Ambidextrous set of hands

Procedure

1. Find a hard surface and give the top a good, fast clockwise spin. Observe what happens.

2. Using this same hard surface, give the top a fast counter-clockwise spin. Make more observations.

Gas Giant #3

How Come, Huh?

The center of mass for this top is not in the exact center of the round part of the top. Instead, it is located slightly above the middle of the sphere. This is because the stem sticks up, and that adjusts the center of mass toward the stem. What this means is that when you spin the top, the forces that are acting on the top are unequal. As the top spins, a torque is placed on the sphere, causing the stem to get nearer and nearer toward the surface it is on. Eventually, the top will wind up spinning on its stem when all of the forces become balanced

The planet Uranus was first discovered in 1781 by William Herschel. About 220 years later, the rings, which are vertical, were discovered when the planet passed in front of a bright star. Voyager 2 flew by in 1986 and discovered that there were moons orbiting this huge planet and, to date, 17 of those moons have been discovered and named.

MASS

In addition to rings and moons that have a vertical orbit, measuring the magnetic field of Uranus has revealed that the core of the planet is off-center, as is shown in the illustration at the left. Like the flipover top, this off-center mass in the planet's interior may be responsible for the tilt of the rings.

Science Fair Extensions

37. Find a large salad bowl in your kitchen, ask for permission to use it for science experiments, and spin the top inside the bowl. Start the top on its side as well as on its base and see what happens.

38. Spin the top on an inclined plane, or ramp, and see if the effect of gravity and the inclined plane affect the way that the top behaves.

39. Using a lump of clay and a thin, cylindrical magnet, create a model of Uranus. Using iron filings, show the position of the magnetic core inside the planet. Also show how the planet is tilted.

Internal Thermal Furnace

The Experiment

Neptune is the eighth planet and the farthest of the four gas giants from the sun. Despite being almost 2.8 million miles from the sun, this planet radiates 2.5 times the amount of heat that it receives from the sun. What this tells astronomers is that Neptune has an internal source of heat. In addition to producing more heat than it absorbs, Neptune has a more turbulent atmosphere than its neighbor, Uranus. This lab will give you an idea of how that heat affects the appearance of this gas giant.

Materials

1   Measuring cup
1   1-oz. bottle of sodium bicarbonate
1   1-oz. bottle of calcium chloride
1   1-oz. bottle of phenol red
1   Resealable baggie
1   Gallon jar
1   Straight pin
    Warm water
    Cold water

Procedure

1. Add a half-cup of warm water to the baggie. If you don't have a measuring cup, fill the bag until there is about an inch of water in it. **(Be sure to use warm water. Using cold water will change the experiment significantly.)**

2. Add half an ounce of phenol red to the baggie of water. The phenol red is an acid/base indicator. However, in this experiment, it allows you to see how the liquid moves.

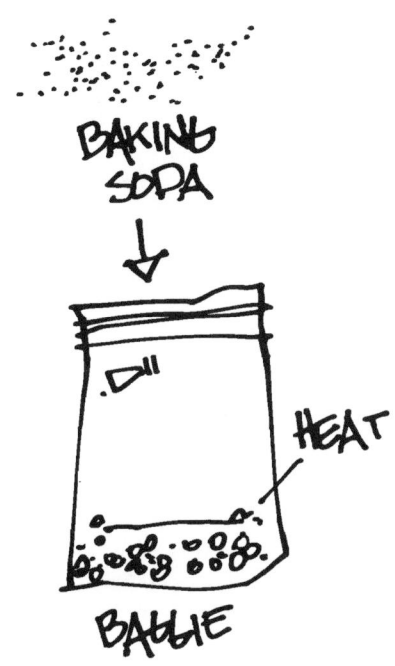

BAKING SODA

HEAT

BAGGIE

3. Fill the gallon jar four-fifths of the way to the top with cold water. Make the water as cold as possible. Set the jar aside.

4. Remove the cap from the calcium chloride bottle and add about one-third of its contents to the water. Zip the baggie closed and roll the calcium chloride pellets between your fingertips.

As the chemical starts to dissolve, you should notice a significant increase in temperature, particularly as you rub the pellets.

5. Using the straight pin, make several holes (four or five) near the top of the baggie.

6. Open the baggie, add one-third of the contents of the bottle of sodium bicarbonate powder, and *quickly* zip the baggie closed again. Gently shove the baggie toward the bottom of the gallon jar. Observe what happens when the chemicals come in contact and react with each other.

JAR

BAGGIE

7. Record what happens to the warm liquid in the baggie when it comes in contact with the cold water in the jar.

Internal Thermal Furnace

Data & Observations

In the space below, draw a picture of how the water in the baggie moves when it comes in contact with the warm water in the jar.

How Come, Huh?

When calcium chloride is mixed with water, it splits apart, forming calcium ions and chloride ions. When this happens, the energy that was holding those atoms together is released as heat. That is why the bag started to feel warm as the reaction proceeded.

Once the chemicals have split apart, each chemical is free to react with other chemicals, like the sodium bicarbonate powder. The chloride reacts with the sodium in the sodium bicarbonate to form table salt and carbon dioxide, which is a gas. A gas takes up more space than a liquid, and this extra gas causes the bag to swell.

As the amount of gas inside the bag increases, the pressure also increases. All of this gas pressure puts considerable strain on the plastic bag that is holding everything inside. As the pressure increases, gas starts to escape from the holes, rising toward the surface of the water in the jar. Eventually, the warm, colored water in the jar also escapes and, due to the difference in temperature, starts to rise toward the surface.

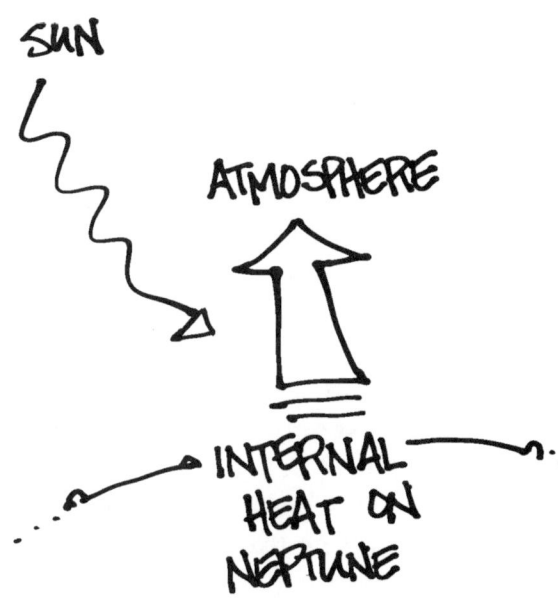

So what does all of this have to do with Neptune, you ask? The heat generated in the chemical reaction is a metaphor for the heat that is produced inside the planet and is radiated out into space. The bubbles of gas and warm water are metaphors for the rising convection currents that stir the atmosphere of Neptune, forming clouds, swirling bands, and the apparent storms that are seen on the blue planet. In fact, winds moving across the frozen methane atmosphere (methane is what gives the planet its blue appearance) have been clocked at speeds in excess of 12,000 mph.

Science Fair Extensions

40. Neptune has moons and rings like the other gas giants. Do some research and find out how many moons there are, whom they were named after, and where they are in relation to the rings.

41. The coldest place in the solar system is located on one of the moons that orbits Neptune. Find out which moon this is and how cold it gets at the polar ice caps.

Pluto and Charon

The Experiment

Congratulations! You made it to the outer reaches of the solar system. If you were actually travelling, you would probably see a sign that says, "Welcome to Pluto!"

Pluto has a companion, a moon called Charon, which has completely synchronized its orbit with that of Pluto. What this means is that the rotation of Pluto and Charon are identical, and if you were standing on the surface of Pluto, you would always see the same side of Charon in the same position in the sky. The other side of Pluto never sees Charon. This lab will help you to understand how this is possible.

Materials

1   # 303 soup can, empty, one end cut out
1   Hammer
1   #16 nail
1   String, 36 inches long
    Water

Procedure

1. Using the hammer and nail, make two small holes near the top of the can, directly opposite each other.

2. Thread the string through the holes and tie it off.

3. Fill the can halfway with water and, working outside or in a large area away from your friends, start to move gently in a circle. As you move in a circle faster and faster, you will notice that as you rotate, the can full of water is also rotating at the exact same cycle as you. (The way you can tell this is that you are able to look down into the can and the top of the can is always facing you.) You and the can have the same period of rotation, just like Pluto and Charon.

How Come, Huh?

So what do whirling cans of water have to do with the last planet in the solar system and its moon? Well, for starters, we can attempt to explain two things: gravity and why the rotational periods of these two bodies always line up facing each other. But, first things first ....

Pluto and Charon

Gravity is a force that pulls objects toward the center of our solar system. It is a powerful force, but it can be overcome by other kinds of forces. When objects spin in a circle, they create a centripetal force that radiates out from the center of the spin. This force pushes objects inward, toward the center of the spin. It is opposed by inertia, which resists the centripetal force and keeps the object in the same place.

If an object is spinning and being pushed away from the center of the spin by inertia, it will continue to move away from the center until it is stopped by another force, usually centripetal force. The centripetal force of the object at any point along the circular path is equal to the tension in the string and the component of the object's weight pointing to the center of the circle. So, if the velocity of the can is great enough, the water won't fall out. This velocity is called the critical speed, and it takes into account the length of the string and the total mass spinning around the center. The string is what is keeping the can in orbit around your head.

Science Fair Extensions

42. Experiment with larger and larger cans of water. See if there is a limit to this experiment and what that limit may be.

43. Try this experiment again, varying the length of the string that is holding the can. Figure out how that affects the experiment, if at all.

44. Replace the water with sand, rocks, pebbles, pancake mix, or carbon dioxide gas. What results do you get, and does it make a difference if the object that you are spinning is a solid, liquid, or gas?

45. Find carnival rides, in particular, those that use circular motion to their advantage, and ride them. Determine the forces that keep you in your seat as you fly upside down.

Big Idea 3

The movements of the sun, Earth, and moon are predictable and regular. These movements produce daily, monthly, and annual phenomena.

Synchronized Sundial

The Experiment

The Earth moves around the sun in a predictable pattern. The sun spins on its axis once every 24 hours, which is how we measure a day, and it rotates around the Earth once every 365 1 / 4 days, which is how we measure a year on Earth.

For many hundreds of years, time was kept using an instrument called a sundial. It was placed in a sunny area and positioned so that, by the location of the shadow, you could tell the time of day. This lab is going to give you an idea of how that is possible.

Materials

2   Wooden metersticks
1   Protractor
1   Grassy area bordering concrete or blacktop
1   Box of chalk
1   Clock

Procedure

1. Find a spot where there is a border between a soft, grassy area and some blacktop or a concrete sidewalk, driveway, or patio. The concrete portion should be running in an east-west direction.

2. At the top of the hour, preferably either 8:00 AM or 9:00 AM, gently insert a meterstick in the soil, right at the edge of the blacktop. Using a piece of chalk, trace the shadow of the meterstick on the ground and write the time at the end of the shadow. Use the illustration on the previous page as a guide.

3. Every hour on the hour, zip outside and locate the shadow. Trace the shadow using a different color of chalk, and write the time at the end of the shadow each time you trace it. Also measure the angle that it has moved with the protractor, and measure the length of the shadow, itself. Both will change constantly. Do this for as long as you are permitted. Try to take readings for at least 8 hours if that is possible. When you are done, fill in the data table below.

Data & Observations

	Time	Shadow Length	Angle Moved
1.			
2.			
3.			
4.			
5.			
6.			
7.			
8.			

Synchronized Sundial

How Come, Huh?

As the Earth spins around its axis and continues its rotation around the sun, the position of the Earth in relation to the sun continually changes.

In the morning, the sun appears to be very low in the sky, casting a long shadow. As the Earth rotates on its axis, your position on the Earth actually becomes closer to the sun. This produces a higher temperature and a shorter shadow. As the Earth continues to rotate, the shadow lengthens again, the degree of change decreases, and the temperature usually decreases.

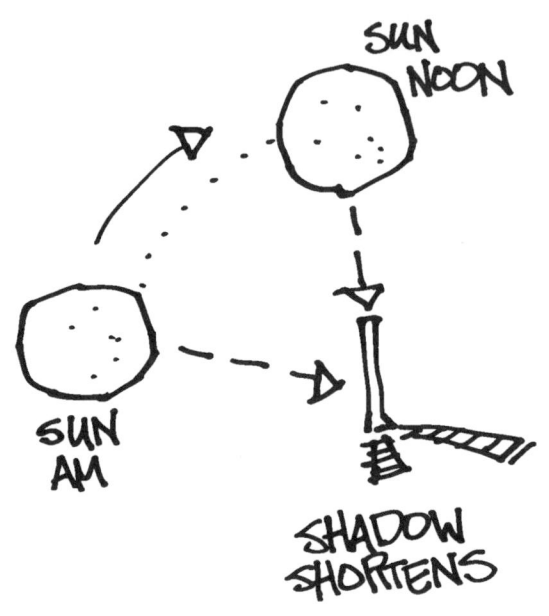

Science Fair Extensions

46. Find a sundial in a community garden, science center, or county park, and take your watch with you. Compare the time reading on the sundial with the reading that you have on your watch. If there is a significant difference, see if you can figure out why.

47. Create a permanent place for your sundial. Take readings every month on the same day of the month, and compare the measurements that you get over a whole year's time.

The Reason for Seasons

The Experiment

If you live on Earth, and presumably you do, and if you also happen to live in North America, you experience seasons to some degree. This lab explores the one simple reason for the seasons—the tilt of the Earth on its axis. As you will see, it is this tilt, coupled with the revolution of the Earth around the sun, that accounts for the coming and going of summer, autumn, winter, and spring.

Materials

1   High-intensity lamp
1   Large table
1   Globe on axis
1   Protractor
2   Liquid crystal thermometers
1   Meterstick
1   Pen or pencil
1   Roll of masking tape

The Reason for Seasons

Procedure

1. Place the meterstick in the middle of a large table. Place a 2-inch strip of masking tape at either end of the meterstick. Rotate the meterstick 90 degrees and place two more 2-inch strips of tape at either end. You should have four strips of tape equidistant from the center of the meterstick. Remove the meterstick and place a fifth piece of tape to mark the center position.

2. On the piece of tape closest to your belly button, write the word *Summer*. The next piece of tape to the right is to be labeled *Autumn*. Then label *Winter* directly across from *Summer*. Finally, label *Spring*.

3. Place the high-intensity lamp on the fifth piece of tape in the middle of the table, pointing toward the piece of tape that says *Summer*. Adjust the lamp so that it is shining directly across the table. Use the illustration on the previous page to help you set this up.

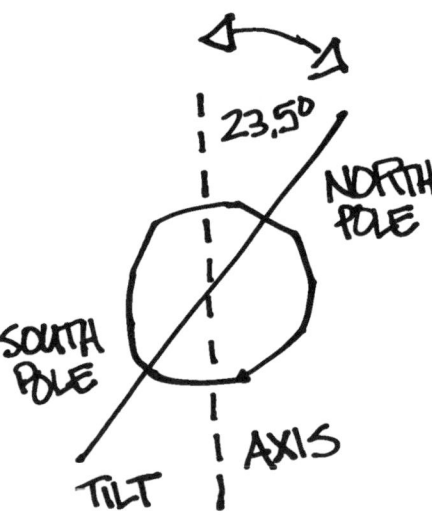

4. Using the globe with the adjustable axis and the protractor, check the tilt of the Earth and make sure that it is 23.5 degrees off center. Use the illustration at the right as a guide.

5. Place the properly tilted globe on the piece of tape that says *Summer*. Rotate the globe so that North America is closest to the sun, and tape one of the liquid crystal thermometers on the 30 degree latitude. Tape the other thermometer the same distance below the Equator, across Argentina and Chile.

6. Allow the globe to be heated by the lamp for five minutes, and then record the temperature in the data table below. Then move the globe to *Spring*, rotate the lamp so that it is shining directly on the Earth, and rotate the globe, keeping the tilt at 23.5 degrees. Shine the lamp on the two LC thermometers for five minutes. Record the temperatures.

7. Continue to rotate the lamp and globe through the other two seasons, recording the temperature each time. When you are done, compare the temperatures with the seasons and see if they follow the natural pattern of changes that we have here on Earth.

Data & Observations

Season	Temp N.A.	Temp S.A.
Summer		
Autumn		
Winter		
Spring		

How Come, Huh?

Due to the tilt of the Earth, North America is closer to the sun in summer and farther from it in winter. The slight difference in distance is enough to account for the changes in temperature that we experience.

Science Fair Extensions

48. All of the planets in the solar system have some degree of tilt. Do some research and make a chart to compare the tilt of each planet to the tilt of the Earth.

Gyro Ring Precession

The Experiment

So, tilt is responsible for the seasons, according to the previous lab. There is a name for this slow-motion wibble-wobbling of all planets and some moons. It is called *precession*. In this lab, we are going to experiment with a fast version of the same thing.

Materials

1   Gyro ring
1   Pair of hands
     Lots of patience and practice

Procedure

1. Hold the gyro ring in either hand. You will notice that the colored washers hang at the bottom of the ring. Keeping your other hand open, whack all of the washers with a quick downward movement. Hit them so that they start to spin around the ring.

2. When you can hit all of the washers and get them spinning fairly quickly, immediately start to rotate the ring in a smooth motion toward you. It may take a couple of tries, but what will eventually happen is the washers will continue to spin as the ring passes through them. With a little bit of practice, you will be able to move the ring through the washers at a speed that allows them to remain spinning as long as you move the ring at a fairly constant speed.

How Come, Huh?

Here's what happens: Think of each washer as a spinning top. The precession, or wobble, of each spinning washer causes one edge of the inner surface of each washer to rub against the steel ring. Due to friction, the point of contact between a washer and the ring acts like a gear. This "gear" transfers energy from the upward motion of the ring to the rotating motion of the washers.

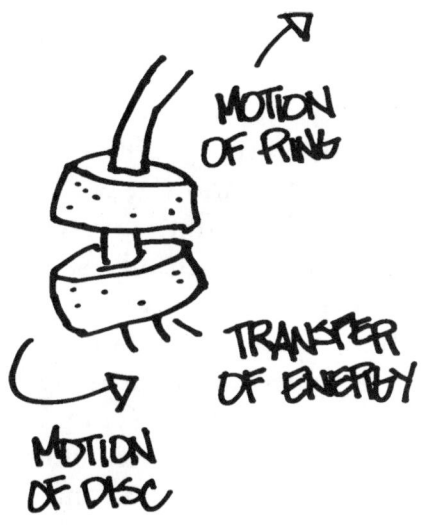

MOTION OF RING

TRANSFER OF ENERGY

MOTION OF DISC

If you speed up the ring, the speed of the washers also speeds up. The Earth's rotation and tilted axis undergo a wobble like that seen in a top or gyroscope. This slow wobble, called precession, takes 26,000 years to complete one cycle and causes the tilt of the Earth's axis to change the direction in which it is pointing. As a result, a January ski vacation to Utah 13,000 years from now will be extremely disappointing, unless you like skiing on bare rock in 80 degree weather.

Science Fair Extensions

49. Rather than give the washers a whack, some folks who make a living selling gyros in mall science and nature stores have perfected a way of starting the washers by simply flipping them with their thumbs.

50. Once you get good at keeping all of the washers spinning, the next skill that you want to master will be flipping the whole gyro into the air and catching it while keeping the washers spinning. Try under-the-leg, behind-the-back, and around-the-neck moves, too. This is not too scientific, but it's a great way to entertain distant relatives and visiting dignitaries.

Down in Front

The Experiment

A total solar eclipse occurs about once a year when light from the sun is blocked by the moon. In order to observe an eclipse, the moon must pass directly between the sun and the place you are standing. Because the eclipse path is a narrow band that can occur anywhere on the Earth's surface, actually seeing an eclipse is a rare, once-in-a-lifetime event, unless you travel to the eclipse path. When you experience an eclipse, the sky appears twilight, just as it does at sunrise or sunset. The colors you would see at the beginning or the end of the day are visible, and birds and other animals tend to be confused.

One of the major problems with watching an eclipse is that people will look directly at the sun while the eclipse is happening. This can cause permanent damage to the eyes. To prevent this damage, you can wear dark welder's goggles, Mylar glasses that you can buy for eclipse viewing, or a sheet of mylar film. The safest way to watch an eclipse is indirectly, using the technique that you will learn and practice in this lab activity.

Materials

2   Index cards
1   Flashlight
1   Thumbtack or pushpin
1   Sheet of black construction paper
1   Pair of scissors
1   Pencil
1   Tennis ball
1   Ping-Pong ball
1   Playground ball

Procedure

1. Make a small pinhole in the center of one of the index cards.

2. Place the bulb-end of the flashlight on the piece of construction paper and trace its outline. Cut out this black disc to use as your moon.

3. Using the illustration at the right, work with your partner and hold the flashlight over the hole in the card so that a complete disc of light is seen on the second index card below.

4. Once you have positioned the flashlight to create the disc of light that represents the sun, you are ready to simulate an eclipse. Have the person who is holding the flashlight slowly move the black paper "moon" across the beam of light. Watch what happens to the disc of light on the bottom index card. Continue to move the paper moon across the front of the lens until it is completely covering the light. Keep going in the same direction until you are past the lens again.

5. Take the Ping-Pong ball (moon), tennis ball (Earth), playground ball (sun), and two friends, and working together, simulate the relative positions of the Earth, moon, and sun, to create a solar eclipse.

Down in Front

Data & Observations

Draw the sequence of what you see as you create your own solar eclipse.

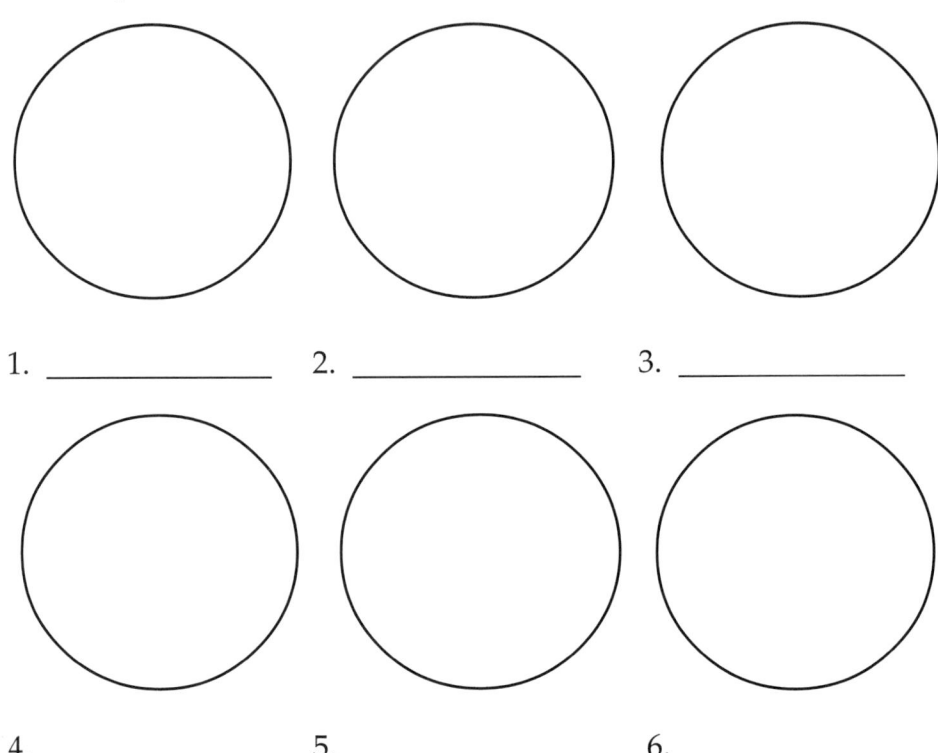

1. _____   2. _____   3. _____

4. _____   5. _____   6. _____

How Come, Huh?

In order for a solar eclipse to occur, the moon must pass directly between the sun and the Earth. When this happens, the shadow of the moon, called the umbra, is smaller than the actual diameter of the Earth, so a total eclipse of the sun is a rare occurrence. Partial eclipses of the sun are more common.

Science Fair Extensions

51. Create a model that allows you to demonstrate a solar eclipse as well as a lunar eclipse. Use the model to explain why lunar eclipses are much more common than solar eclipses.

52. There is a fair amount of folklore associated with lunar and solar eclipses. Do some research and find out what the ancient myths and stories regarding the occurrences of eclipses are, and how eclipses affected the civilizations that witnessed them.

53. Do some research and find out how many moons orbit the other planets. If you know the rate of the orbit of each moon, you can predict the frequency of lunar and solar eclipses. (Just think of the comings and goings of astral phenomena on Saturn, which has at least 18 moons.)

Moon Tracker

The Experiment

The moon goes zipping all over the place, all of the time. A great activity to illustrate how the moon moves through the night sky is to draw a picture of your neighborhood horizon and then track the movement of the moon, relative to buildings, trees, and water towers every half-hour for several hours.

Materials

1   Drawing pad
3   Colored pencils
1   Clear, moonless night

Procedure

1. Head outside on a clear, winter's evening. Winter is best because the sun goes down sooner and the moon is easier to see. Pick a period of time around the full moon. Your local newspaper usually will print the days for the full, partial, and new moons.

2. Pick an early start time, preferably 5:30 PM or earlier, and draw a sketch of your neighborhood skyline. Include trees, buildings, powerlines, water towers, mountains, and any other distinguishing features. Then, when your drawing is complete, locate the moon and draw it on your horizon. Label the time next to your moon.

3. Every half-hour for at least 3 hours, head outside, locate your moon, and draw a picture of where the moon is located and how big it appears. Be sure to record the time of each drawing. As the evening progresses, you should be able to see a definite pathway along which the moon is traveling.

4. Wait one week and head outside again at the exact same time, and record the position of the moon a second time in a second color of pencil. Compare the location of the moon, the path that it travels, and its size and shape, as well.

5. Repeat this one more time, two weeks later, with yet another colored pencil. Compare the results with those that you recorded during the previous two weeks.

How Come, Huh?

The moon will appear larger near the horizon in the early evening. The reason for this is that the light reflected from the surface of the moon must pass through more of the Earth's atmosphere. The molecules in the atmosphere bend the light, causing the moon to appear larger than it really is.

Science Fair Extensions

54. Grab a telescope or pair of good binoculars and examine the surface of the moon. You will see oceans, seas, craters, and mountains, but they will not be much like the ones we have here on Earth. Compare what you see with a map of the moon, and see if you can find the moon's prominent features.

Lunar Phases

The Experiment

It is probably a safe assumption that most astronomers are always aware of the current phase of the moon. The reason for this is that astronomers do not get very much work done during a full moon because there is too much light in the night sky. This happens every 29 1/2 days, as the moon completes a cycle. A new moon is dark and can't be seen very well at all, while a full moon is a complete disc of light and can be seen quite easily in the sky. In between these two phases are several others that you will model in this lab activity.

Materials

1   Ball (softball-sized or larger)
1   Flashlight
1   Partner

Procedure

1. You will recreate the positions of the sun, moon, and Earth that create the different phases of the moon. One person holds the sun (the flashlight) and shines it toward the Earth (a second student). The Earth then holds the ball directly out in front, between herself and the sun and the Earth. The illustration on the next page will help you figure out where everything should go.

2. In the first circle in the *Data & Observations* section, draw a picture of what the moon looks like as seen from the Earth. Indicate how much of the illuminated portion of the moon can be seen from Earth by shading in the area that appears dark to the "Earth person" holding the ball.

3. With the sun still shining on the moon, have the Earth hold the moon in her left hand and move her arm 45 degrees to the left. Observe how much of the illuminated side of the moon can now be seen from the Earth. Record the Earth person's observations by shading as required in circle number 2.

4. Repeat the previous step, with the Earth holding the moon straight out to the left at 90 degrees. Record the Earth person's observations in circle number 3.

5. You should have the idea by now, so continue around the circle to the left in 45-degree intervals until you have recorded data for all 8 positions. The Earth person will have to rotate as she moves the moon around so she can see the moon when it revolves around behind her.

One more hint is in order. When the moon is directly opposite the Earth from the sun, make sure the Earth person holds the moon high enough so her head and body don't block the sun. If she doesn't, you will end up with a very funky eclipse.

Lunar Phases

Data & Observations

Record your observations of the moon in eight different phases.

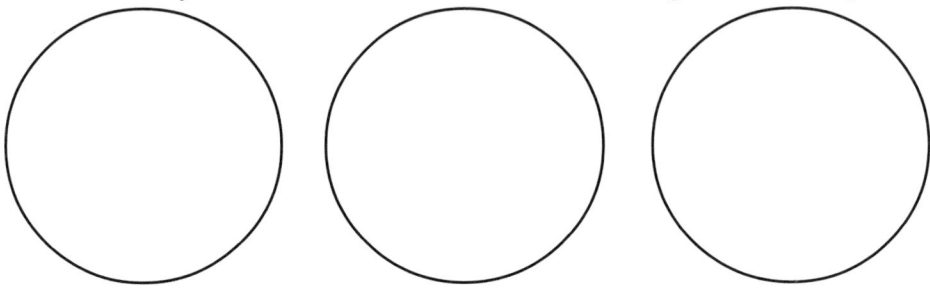

1. _____   2. _____   3. _____

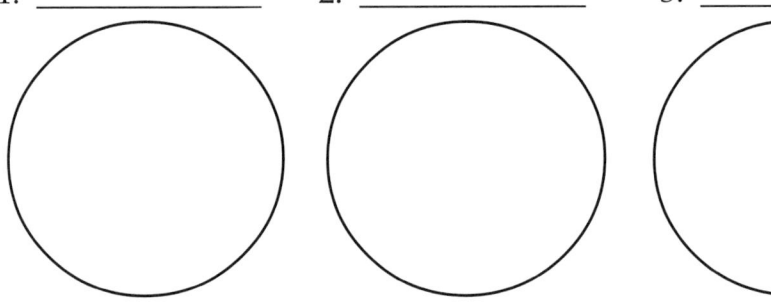

4. _____   5. _____   6. _____

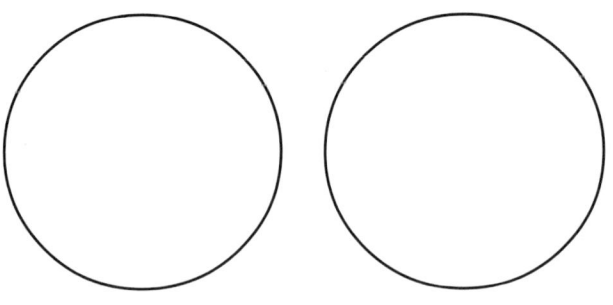

7. _____   8. _____

How Come, Huh?

The moon revolves around the Earth every 29 1/2 days. During this rotation, the position of the moon varies each night and, as it passes through the shadow of the Earth, some or all of the light coming from the sun is blocked out.

Science Fair Extensions

55. Compare the phases of the moon with the phases of Venus, and note the similarities and differences between the two. Explain two reasons why this same effect could not be observed with Mars.

56. Create your own Earth-moon-sun model that rotates. Using this model, show the different phases of the moon, a lunar eclipse, and a solar eclipse.

Lunar Eclipse

The Experiment

A total lunar eclipse occurs about once a year when light from the sun is blocked by the Earth. In order to observe an eclipse, the Earth must pass directly between the sun and the Moon. This lab will give you an opportunity to create the circumstances that allow a lunar eclipse to be seen.

Materials

1   Tennis ball
1   Ping-Pong ball
1   Playground ball

Procedure

Using the model that is illustrated below, use the Ping-Pong ball (moon), tennis ball (Earth), playground ball (sun), and two friends. Working together, simulate the relative positions of the Earth, moon, and sun to create a lunar eclipse.

SUN

EARTH

MOON

Big Idea 4

The moon and Earth have many characteristics—some that are shared with other planets and moons and some that are unique.

Crater Construction

The Experiment

When you have a chance to sit and just look at the moon with your peepers, you can actually see that the surface appears irregular. We are guessing that is how the "Man in the Moon" myth got started. If you have the opportunity to look at the night sky with a pair of binoculars and tune in to the surface of the moon, you will see mountains, seas, and most visibly, craters.

The craters are formed by meteors and meteorites that crash into the surface of the moon, displacing large piles of rock and dust that are found on the surface. This lab will give you an idea of how this happens.

Materials

1   Bag of marbles
       (various sizes)
1   Box of fine sand
1   Soda pop box lid
1   Chair

Procedure

1. Fill the soda pop box with 2 inches of sand and set it at the base of the chair.

2. Stand on the chair and hold the bag of marbles. Drop the marbles from various heights into the sand.

3. When you are all done, gently remove the marbles from the craters that they have made, and draw a picture of the pattern that was created. Compare it with a picture of the surface of the moon in a book.

Data & Observations

Draw a picture of the crater pattern that you created.

How Come, Huh?

Craters are formed the same way on the surface of the moon as they were formed in this lab. Objects hurl in from space and, not having an atmosphere to contend with, zip right on down to the surface of the moon, making their impressions on the local neighborhood.

Science Fair Extensions

57. Try other materials. Ash from a fireplace is very effective but also very messy. Fine, dusty powder from some of the more arid regions of the west work well, and, of course, you could always check out a pile of moon dust from NASA. (Just kidding. Please don't call NASA and ask to borrow their samples.)

Moon v. Earth

The Objective

Listed below are features of the moon, of the Earth, and of *both* the moon and the Earth. Your job is to do a little bit of research, use some common sense, and check the appropriate boxes to show which characteristics belong to which planets.

Data Table

Found on Moon	Feature	Found on Earth
	Water	
	Soil	
	Rocks	
	Atmosphere	
	Plants	
	Animals	
	Clouds	
	Craters	
	Mountains	
	Gravity	
	Meteorites	
	Microbes	
	Canyons	
	Fungus	
	Wind	
	Glaciers	
	Oceans	

How Come, Huh?

The main difference between the Earth and the moon is that the Earth is very adept at supporting life, and the moon comes up short in that category. The most obvious difference is the lack of an atmosphere. The second is the absence of water. Cure those two little problems and things could pick up significantly.

Science Fair Extensions

58. There are many, many moons in our solar system. Start with the two zipping around Mars, pick up speed (and moons) as you count the 18 from Saturn, 17 from Jupiter, 15 from Uranus, Neptune's 10, and Pluto's partner in crime, Charon, and you have quite a few moons. Create a list of characteristics, sizes, shapes, orbits, volcanic activity, and colors, and make a list of comparisons of moons in the solar system. See how the different moons stack up.

Evidence of Atmosphere

The Experiment

The Earth is surrounded by an atmosphere. This is not unique to the solar system; other planets have atmospheres. However, others don't have atmospheres made up of nitrogen and oxygen. We have about 100 miles of this nitrogen/oxygen-gas-mix stacked on top of us, and this creates a lot of pressure—almost 15 pounds per square inch, which we will use to infer the presence of an atmosphere.

In this lab, we'll use a fake mosquito to show some of the effects of pressure on all of us on Earth. The fanny of this "mosquito" is heated in a propane flame. When the proboscis of the "mosquito" is inverted into a cup of blood-red liquid and it is instructed to take a drink, the tube fills rapidly with the red liquid. That's pressure for you!

Materials

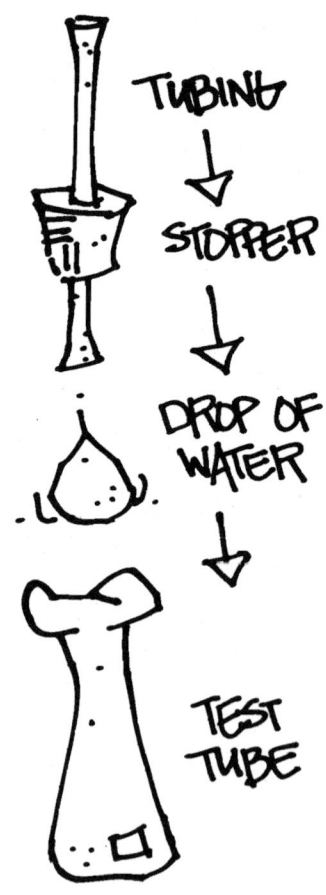

1 Pyrex test tube, 20 x 150
1 #1 One-hole stopper
1 8-inch piece of 3 mm glass tubing
1 Propane torch
2 Test tube clamps
1 Book of matches
1 Cup with water
1 Bottle of liquid soap
1 Pair of goggles
1 Bottle of white glue
1 Bottle of red food coloring
2 "Eyes" from a craft store
   Masking tape
   Adult Supervision

Procedure

1. Dip the end of the glass tubing in the bottle of soap. This will make the glass slippery so that you can slide it into the rubber stopper easily.

2. When the glass tubing is inserted into the stopper, glue two eyes to the front of the stopper. Clip the two test tube clamps onto the tube so that they look like wings. Use the illustration to the right as a guide.

3. To make your "blood," fill the cup with water and add several drops of red food coloring. (To darken your blood and give it a deeper, more realistic color, add blue food coloring, a drop at a time.) If you are doing this as a demonstration for your friends, you may want to label the cup "blood sample," using a piece of masking tape.

4. Add a drop of water to the bottom of the Pyrex test tube. This accelerates the rate of the experiment and also gives you an easy measure of when to invert the tube into the liquid. Flip the mosquito upside down in the "blood" and instruct it to drink. When nothing happens, tell your friends that sometimes you have to "encourage" the mosquito to drink, so you are going to heat its fanny.

5. Put on your goggles, and with the supervision of an adult, light the propane torch and heat the bottom of the tube. You placed a drop of water in the tube, so keep an eye on that drop. When it boils and produces steam, the mosquito is ready to drink the blood. Invert the tube and stick the glass tubing into the sample of "blood." Observe what happens.

Evidence of Atmosphere

Data & Observations

In the spaces provided below, draw a picture of what happened when the mosquito was given a drink of blood before and after its bottom was heated.

How Come, Huh?

The first time you inverted the tube, the air pressure inside and outside the tube was equal, so there was no movement. As you heated the tube, the air molecules inside the tube started getting very excited and were bouncing around and off one another. This heating caused the air inside the tube to expand, and quite a few of the air molecules actually left the tube.

When the tube was flipped over a second time and the glass tube was inserted into the water, you created a closed system. Nothing could get in or out of the tube. The air pressure outside the tube pushing on the water was the same as before, but as the tube cooled, the few remaining air molecules didn't take up very much space, which created low pressure inside the tube.

This low pressure did not provide much resistance, so the air outside **pushed** the water up into the tube. As you can see from the amount of water that was allowed inside the tube, there was very little air left inside after the heating.

Differences in air pressure are responsible for winds being created, huge storm systems being formed, and entertaining physics experiments.

Science Fair Extensions

59. Experiment with the diameter of the tube and see if there is a difference in the way the experiment comes to life. In particular, does the diameter of the mosquito's proboscis make it easier or harder to drink the blood as the diameter gets wider?

60. Set up an experiment to see if the volume of the mosquito's fanny makes a difference. You started with a Pyrex tube. What happens if you use a larger tube? How about a smaller one? Change the shape of the tube by substituting an Erlenmeyer flask or a boiling flask.

Tabletop Borealis

The Experiment

The sun emits bazillions of charged particles that radiate out into the universe. When these charged particles hit the Earth's magnetosphere (explained in a couple of labs), they are "guided" toward the North and South Poles, where they burn up, producing showers of colors in the Earth's atmosphere.

Spectroscopes have a special film called diffraction grating that acts like a prism to separate light into its colors. Different elements combine to make different light sources. These different combinations of elements make patterns of color, called line spectra, that are unique to different light sources. By using diffraction grating, you will learn about identifying different light sources by their "fingerprints." This information is useful in determining star age, star composition, and just exactly which particles are bombarding the Earth as they create these spectacular displays of light.

Materials

1   Propane torch
1   Nichrome wire
1   Bottle of 10% hydrochloric acid
1   Bottle of strontium chloride solution
1   Commercial spectroscope
1   Bottle of potassium chloride solution
1   Bottle of barium chloride solution
1   Box of colored pencils
    Adult Supervision

Procedure

1. With the assistance and supervision of an adult, light the propane torch.

2. Dip the nichrome wire into the diluted hydrochloric acid. While the wire is wet, dip it into the strontium chloride and then place the wire in the flame of the torch. Observe the color that is produced and record it in the *Data* section on the next page.

3. Darken the room and repeat the procedure of burning the strontium in the flame, only this time, look at the colors through the spectroscope. The diffraction grating will produce thin lines of different colors. Try your very best to determine how many lines of each color are produced and where they are located. Record your observations.

4. Repeat the procedure for the other two chemicals and record your observations in the *Data & Observations* section.

Tabletop Borealis

Data & Observations

Draw a picture of the color bands that you saw through the spectroscope when each chemical was ignited.

Colors Seen Through Spectroscope

┌──┐
│   │
│   │
└──┘

Strontium Chloride

┌──┐
│   │
│   │
└──┘

Potassium Chloride

┌──┐
│   │
│   │
└──┘

Barium Chloride

How Come, Huh?

Astronomers use the light received through spectroscopes to learn about objects in space. This light carries information about stars' temperatures, composition, magnetic fields, and motion. This information is decoded by splitting the light into a spectrum, using a spectroscope. The bright line spectrum that results is often called an emission spectrum, or a characteristic spectrum. Every atom has an individual and characteristic spectrum, much like every person has a fingerprint that can be used for identification because it is like no one else's.

When the sun emits charged particles during solar prominences, sun spots, and other occurrences, these charged particles travel through space. When they come near the Earth, the magnetosphere either repels or attracts the charged particles. Those that are attracted enter the Earth's atmosphere at very high speeds and burn up when they encounter the friction produced by the air. As they burn up, like the chemicals introduced into the flame, they ignite and produce colors representative of the elements of which they are composed. The aurora borealis is a spectacular display of the fact that the Earth is surrounded by an atmosphere that contains oxygen.

Science Fair Extensions

61. Some of the science supply companies carry tubes full of gases that can be excited (meaning made to glow) using an electric current. When these tubes are plugged in, you can view them through a spectroscope and see the characteristic bands that are produced by specific chemicals. Mix and view combinations of the tubes to show how these fingerprints can be used in identifying substances.

62. Test some common elements and identify their color band fingerprints. Ask a friend to mix various combinations of these chemicals, and see if you can correctly identify the mixtures that have been put together.

Zip, Drip, & Splash

The Experiment

Earth has water in solid, liquid, and gas forms. Not only that, but water is constantly being recycled—a very unique property of our planet. In this lab, you are going to feel radiant heat, see water evaporating, and observe the condensation of warm, moist air due to changes in temperature. The collective accumulation of water into large drops succumbs to the pleadings of gravity as the drops fall back into the "ocean" of water, also known as a saucepan.

Materials

1   Quart saucepan
    Ice cubes
    Water
1   Hotplate or stove
1   Metal cookie sheet
1   Plastic tub, 5-quart size or larger
1   Water cycle guide (See *Data & Observations* section.)
    Adult Supervision

Procedure

1. Fill the saucepan completely with water. With an adult nearby, turn the hotplate or stove on and start to heat the water to boiling.

2. While the water is heating, place 30 to 40 ice cubes on top of the cookie sheet. The ice cubes will cool the temperature of the sheet significantly.

3. When the water starts to boil, hold the cookie sheet over the evaporating water. Use the illustration on the prvious page as a guide. Observe what happens to the water vapor as it hits the cookie sheet.

4. When you are all done, use the illustrations below and on the next page to create a Mini Water Cycle Poster. Cut or copy the illustrations, place them in their proper sequence, color, and add text to explain what is happening at each step in the process.

Data & Observations

Use these illustrations to create a poster.

RUNOFF

WATER EVAPORATES

Zip, Drip, & Splash

RADIANT ENERGY

PRECIPITATION

How Come, Huh?

Here's how this lab breaks down into the parts of the water cycle:

Radiant Energy: The hotplate does the work of the sun, providing heat to the water so that it evaporates and rises.

Evaporation: The hot, moist air is expanding and rising the same way that water heated by the sun rises as a vapor into the atmosphere.

Condensation: When the warm air hits the bottom of the cookie sheet, it quickly cools. If you look carefully, sometimes you can see a thin layer of "cloud" near the bottom of the sheet. The water molecules continue to cool and accumulate into large water drops on the bottom of the pan. When they finally get too heavy to hang onto the bottom of the pan, we have …

Precipitation: Rain. The rain falls back into the pan and the process, as with nature, starts all over again.

Science Fair Extensions

63. Models can always be improved. Create a detailed model that has mountains, a river to collect water, and a big puddle or small ocean to refill.

Compass in a Cup

The Experiment

The center of the Earth is a huge ball of nickel and iron. Both of these materials are magnetic and, in combination, they produce a very strong magnetic field that not only affects things on Earth but also surrounds the Earth with a shield called the magnetosphere, protecting it from harmful particles and rays. This is a characteristic of our planet that is shared with several other planets in the solar system.

In this lab, with just a couple of simple materials, you will be able to turn an ordinary drinking cup into a compass. This compass will detect and display the presence of the magnetic field that is surrounding the Earth. Sounds mystical, but it isn't.

Materials

1   Index card
1   Pair of scissors
1   Steel sewing needle
1   Thread, 12 inches long
1   Pencil
1   Drinking glass
1   Bar magnet
1   Compass
1   Sheet of paper
1   Pencil

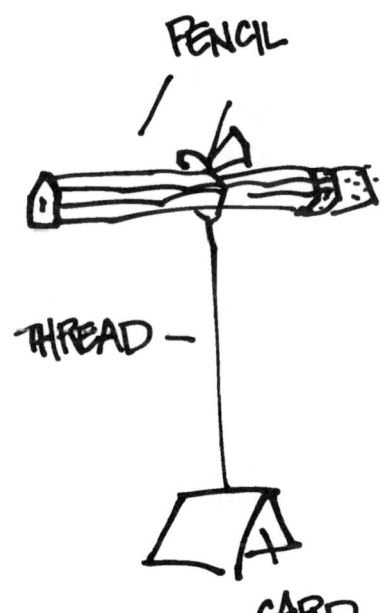

Procedure

1. Take the index card, fold it in half, and using the needle, pierce a small hole into the center of the fold.

2. Wiggle one end of the thread through the hole. Double-knot the other end and gently pull it up to the hole.

Compass in a Cup

3. Tie the loose end of the thread around the middle of the pencil. Hold the index card in the drinking glass and wind the thread up so that the card is in the middle, hanging freely in the glass.

4. Stroke the sewing needle with the north end of the bar magnet about 50 times. We use the word *stroke* instead of *rub* because it is important that you lift the magnet up at the end of each stroke and place it back at the top of the needle.

Think of combing your hair. You would not stick your comb or brush on your head and run it back and forth. You comb or brush in one direction to organize the hair shafts. You are doing the same thing with the iron particles in the needle.

5. Slide the needle into the card. Lower the card into the glass and let the needle orient with the magnetic field of the Earth.

Compare the position of *your* compass with the position of the needle on your commercially prepared compass.

6. Slide a sheet of paper under the glass and mark the direction for *North* on the paper. Rotate the cup about 90 degrees to the left and watch to see what happens to the needle. Check to make sure that it reorients itself toward north.

How Come, Huh?

The iron particles in the needle were organized and lined up when you stroked the needle with the magnet. This magnetized the needle. When the needle was free to move in the glass, the magnetic field of the Earth influenced the needle and caused it to align with the North and South Poles of the Earth.

When you moved the glass off-center, the needle, under the influence of the Earth's magnetic field, rotated back into alignment. The Earth contains a giant, powerful magnet in its core. The magnet produces a magnetic field that surrounds the Earth and extends into space for millions of miles. This magentic field, when it is out in space, is called the magneto-sphere. As charged particles from the sun come in contact with the magnetosphere, like charges are repelled out and around the Earth and opposite-charged particles are attracted to the poles of the Earth. The particles enter the atmosphere, bump into one too many air molecules, and ignite, converting their chemical energy to light energy and producing an amazingly beautiful phenomenon.

Science Fair Extensions

64. Fill the glass with water and try suspending the needle in that medium. Do you get the same results or does the water impede, or interfere with, the movement of the needle?

Iron Filing Maps

The Experiment

A single compass allows you to detect the magnetic field of the Earth and see where those lines of force are pointing, but it does not really give you the whole picture. To actually see the entire magnetic field, you would need either a huge pile of very small compasses or the next best thing—a pile of iron filings.

This lab will allow you create a picture of the magnetic field surrounding three different magnets by using a thin layer of iron filings. These are similar to the magnetic field surrounding the Earth.

Materials

1   Bottle of iron filings
1   Shoebox lid
1   Pair of scissors
1   Sheet of plastic wrap
1   Roll of tape
1   Donut magnet
1   Cow magnet
1   Magnetic wand
1   Bar magnet
1   Pencil

Procedure

1. To make your magnetic field viewer, begin by cutting the center from the lid of the shoebox. Flip the shoebox lid upside down, place a square of plastic wrap on the inside of the lid, and tape it in place. Flip the shoebox lid over, and you are ready to go.

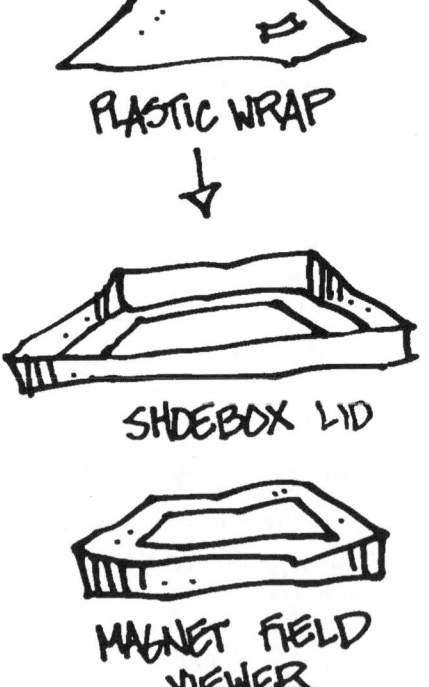

PLASTIC WRAP

SHOEBOX LID

MAGNET FIELD VIEWER

2. Place a magnet under the shoebox lid, centering it in the cellophane window. Once the magnet is centered, sprinkle iron filings all over the top of the lid. Be generous; you will be able to recycle them.

3. Once you have the filings on the lid, gently tap the edge of the box, and the filings will align in the natural pattern of the lines of force.

4. Draw a picture of the magnetic field for each of the three magnets on separate sheets of paper.

5. Notice that the general direction of the compass needles that you observed in the previous lab and the pattern and direction of the iron filings should be very similar to each other.

6. When you are done with the first magnet, all you have to do is lift the box lid up and remove the magnet. Then replace it with the next one that you want to investigate. No mess. Repeat this procedure for the other three magnets.

Data & Observations

On a separate sheet of paper, draw a picture of the magnetic field of the cow magnet. Trace the outline of the next magnet that you are experimenting with and then draw the magnetic field as revealed by the iron filings. Replicate the magnetic field around the cow magnet on a separate sheet of paper.

Iron Filing Maps

How Come, Huh?

Each iron filing is a miniature magnet or compass, with a north and south pole. The magnet influences the filings, and they move to reflect the lines of force coming from the magnet. By tapping on the edge of the box, you are simply aligning the iron filings along the pathways created by the magnetic field.

The cow magnet should have created magnetic field patterns. The donut magnet is another creature altogether. It is created by taking a long tube magnet and slicing it like a loaf of bread. Because the magnet has already been generated when the slicing takes place, this leaves a north pole on one side of the magnet and a south pole on the other side. When you place it on top of the paper, you are literally taking an end view of the top of the magnet—not a side view, like you were taking with the other magnets.

Science Fair Extensions

65. There are several magnets that we have left uninvited to the party. Try horseshoe magnets, book magnets, bar magnets, disc magnets, and lodestone, for starters.

Magnetic Soap Bubbles

The Experiment

A rubber balloon will be rubbed on someone's head, preferably someone with fine shoulder-length hair. As the electrons gang up on the surface of the balloon, the hair will begin to wig out. You can also stick the balloon to the ceiling, walls, passing secretaries, or wool sweaters. The same balloon has a very interesting effect on soap bubbles that happen to be floating around the room. You'll find that the balloon will attract the soap bubbles.

The astronomy tie-in here is that the sun produces literally countless charged particles that are emitted during solar prominences, solar flares, sun spot activity, and other forms of celestial heartburn. These particles ride the solar wind out into the galaxy and some of them, in the process, encounter the Earth's magnetosphere. This magnetosphere tends to have the same effect on the charged particles that the balloon has on the bubbles. Lab time.

Materials

1 Rubber balloon
1 Volunteer (The cat will also do, in a pinch.)
1 Bottle of bubble solution

Procedure

1. Inflate the balloon. If this is hard to do, have someone lend you a lung.

Magnetic Soap Bubbles

2. Select a volunteer. For best results, use someone who has shoulder-length hair that is free of mousse, hairspray, or gel. Fine hair tends to work better than coarse hair. This experiment works best on a dry day—the lower the humidity, the better. And remember, blondes may have more fun, but not until you rub their heads.

Rub the balloon all over the volunteer's head. As you rub, occasionally lift the balloon up off the hair about 6 inches. The hair will follow. After about 30 seconds of rubbing, the hair should be sticking up all around.

3. Have another person blow bubbles. Hold the charged balloon near the soap bubbles and you will find that you can tug the bubbles all over the classroom with the balloon.

4. You will have to practice to get good at this. As soon as the bubbles encounter the static charge on the balloon, they will accelerate toward the balloon. Needless to say, if a bubble hits the balloon, it will pop. The technique that works best for us is to use the same motion that you use when you are hooking a fish. As the bubble approaches the balloon, lift the balloon quickly to separate it from the bubble a bit. The bubble will "lose" the charge temporarily, and you can bring the balloon back down toward the bubble again. When you find the right distance, you can pull the bubble all over the room.

How Come, Huh?

Opposite charges (negative and positive) attract, and like charges (negative and negative) or (positive and positive) repel, or drive apart. The balloon has a huge negative charge because it has stolen all these loose electrons. The hair has a huge positive charge because all of its electrons have been stolen. Balloon negative, hair positive; they attract. When you take the balloon out of the picture, the hair still tends to stand up on end. This is because each of the hair strands has a positive charge. Like charges repel, and because they can't stand each other, they get as far away from each other as possible. In this case, they stand on end.

The bubble is attracted to the static charge on the balloon because our water molecule has one side that is positively charged and one side that is negatively charged. Opposites attract.

The same kind of attraction happens in space. The magnetosphere extends out from the Earth, forming a kind of barrier. When the charged particles hit this barrier, they are either repelled back out into the solar wind and go around the Earth or they are directed into the Van Allen belts and head for the North or South Poles. When this happens, the particles enter the Earth's atmosphere and are burned up upon entry, producing the aurora borealis.

Science Fair Extensions

66. There are lots of items that will hold an electrostatic charge. Experiment with rabbit fur, a fluorescent tube, a glass rod that has been charged with a piece of wool, and anything else that you think may attract soap bubbles.

Big Idea 5

The sun is a star that has all of the characteristics of other stars in our universe.

Solar Features

The Ideas

Our sun is a medium-sized star about halfway through its life expectancy. It is as large as 300,000 Earths stacked into a huge pile and has a surface temperature of roughly 5,800 degrees Kelvin. It rotates once every 25 days and is surrounded by a magnetic field, like the Earth only a bit bigger. This section will introduce you to a couple of features.

SUN

Details

Sunspots

Sunspots are areas on the sun's surface that are cooler than the surrounding areas. They usually come in clusters of no fewer than 10 and as many as 100 in a group. They tend to follow an 11-year cycle where they peak and then almost disappear. It is believed that sunspot activity is related to solar flares that are seen on the surface of the sun.

SUNSPOTS

Solar Flare

The most violent event on the surface of the sun is called a solar flare. Astronomers believe that these flares, also called Coronal Mass Ejections, are caused when magnetic fields on the sun collide. These collisions produce flares of protons and electrons that explode millions of miles out into space.

SOLAR FLARE

Solar Features

ECLIPSE

Eclipse
An eclipse of the sun is produced when the moon comes between the sun and the Earth. The moon partially blocks the rays of sunlight coming from the star as it passes in front of the observer. There are partial solar eclipses frequently, but full solar eclipses are very rare and will happen only a couple of times during a person's lifetime.

CORONA

Corona
The corona is an invisible magnetic field that surrounds the surface of the sun. It fluctuates in size and shape. The most obvious effect of the sun's corona is the solar wind that is produced when charged particles are pushed away from the sun. When the charged particles of the solar wind strike the atmosphere of the Earth, they burn up, producing bright colors called an aurora borealis.

How Come, Huh?
This section gives you a brief introduction to important solar features.

Science Fair Extensions
67. The best time to view a solar corona is during an eclipse. Find out the proper ways to view an eclipse and figure out just why this astral event provides so much information about this one feature of a star.

Homemade 'Scope

The Experiment

A spectroscope is an instrument that collects a small sample of light at one end and then splits that sample with a piece of diffraction grating at the other end. As the light sample passes through the diffraction grating, it separates into specific bands of light. This sequence is unique to every element and compound, and it provides a fingerprint of that element that can later be used to identify mystery compounds. Astronomers use this information to study light coming from stars, and with that light, they can determine the age of a star, its composition, and how fast it is moving away from the Earth, as well as several other tidbits of info.

In this experiment, you are going to make your own spectroscope using a toilet paper tube, aluminum foil, and diffraction grating. Once you have completed the spectroscope, you are going to examine several light sources, but remember to NEVER look directly at the SUN.

Materials

1   Toilet paper tube
1   Rubberband
1   Sheet of aluminum foil, 4 inches by 4 inches
1   Pair of scissors
1   Penknife or dissecting scalpel
1   Piece of diffraction grating
1   Source of light

Procedure

1. Take the toilet paper tube and cut a narrow slot in one end. The slot should go almost all the way through the tube.

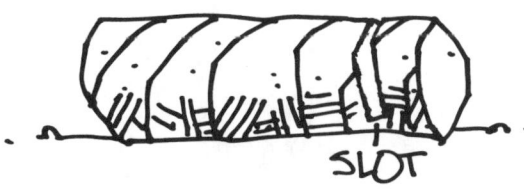

SLOT

Homemade 'Scope

2. Place the aluminum foil over the end opposite the cut in the tube, and fix it in place with the rubberband. Make a narrow slit in the aluminum foil with the knife or dissecting scalpel.

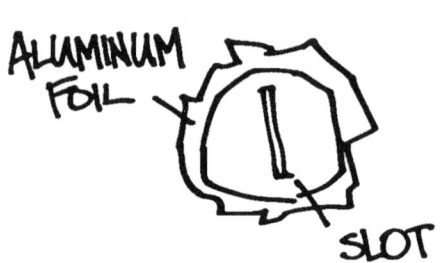

3. Slide the diffraction grating into the slit that you created in step 1.

4. Turn the flashlight on and shine the light toward the slit in the aluminum foil. Look at the back of the diffraction grating and see if a pattern is produced.

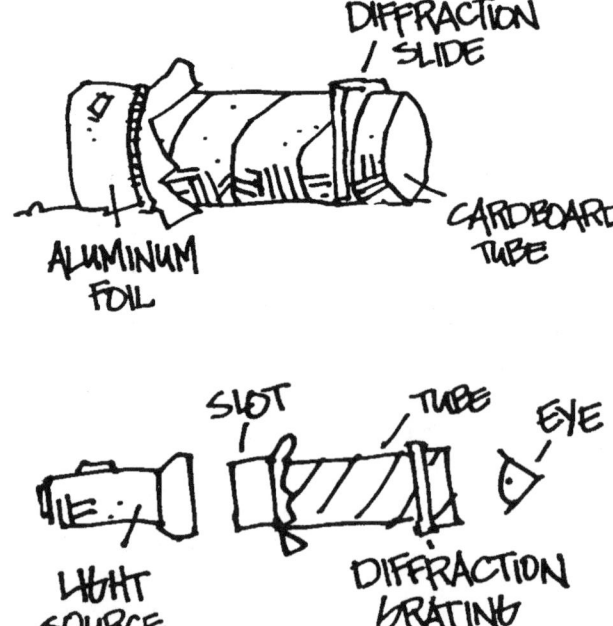

There are a couple of things you can do if you do not see specific bands of light. One, make sure the slit in the aluminum foil is either perfectly vertical or horizontal to the diffraction grating. Also, taking the diffraction grating out and rotating it 90 degrees sometimes helps.

This is science; sometimes you are going to have to tweak your equipment a little bit before it performs the way you want it to.

Data & Observations

Draw a picture of the line spectrum that you see when looking at the flashlight through your spectroscope.

How Come, Huh?

As the light strikes the slit at the end of the tube, only a small amount makes it to the diffraction grating. This sliver of light is then sorted by the color lines in the grating, producing the line spectrum.

Science Fair Extensions

68. Once you get the hang of it, design several other kinds of spectroscopes and build them. Rate their performance, figure out their weaknesses, and show a history of development for each one.

Sunspot Convective Zones

The Experiment

If you could slice open our sun or any other star for that matter, you would see that it has several features. The main idea that we are going work with is the idea of a supergranule. This is a convection cell located near the surface of the sun.

In this particular experiment, we are going to recommend a commercially produced glass tube that we have available in our catalog and on our website. The tube looks like a fat "O" and has an opening at the top where you add water and a drop of food coloring. Aside from the opening, the shape of the convection tube is very similar to the shape and behavior of a supergranule.

Once the tube is filled, you light a votive candle— adult supervision, as always, is recommended—and you heat one side of the "O." As the water is heated, it starts to flow in a convection current.

Materials

1   Convection tube
1   Votive candle
1   Bottle of food coloring
    Water
    Adult Supervision

Procedure

1. Fill the convection tube with room temperature water. Add two or three drops of food coloring to one side of the convection tube and try not to disturb the food coloring.

2. Hold the side of the tube that has the food coloring directly over the candle flame. Use the illustration at the left as a guide.

3. Observe what happens as the water on that side of the tube is heated.

How Come, Huh?

As the water was heated, it absorbed the energy from the burning candle. This caused the molecules of water to move back and forth and bounce around more than the molecules of water that were not being heated by the candle. All this bouncing around caused the same number of molecules to take up more space. This makes the water less dense.

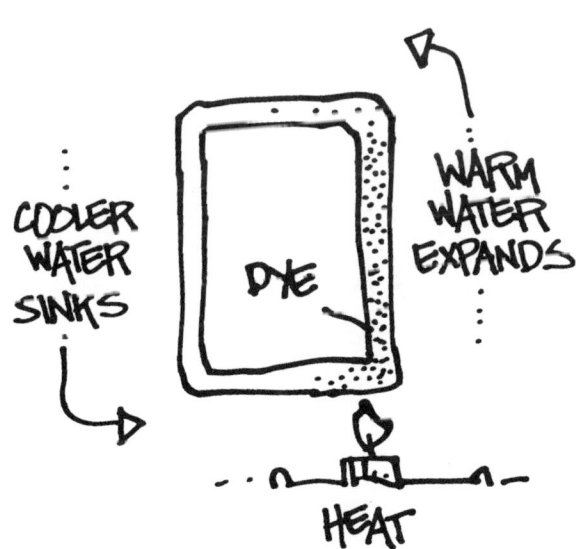

COOLER WATER SINKS

DYE

WARM WATER EXPANDS

HEAT

Sunspot Convective Zones

The less dense water was lighter than the cold water, and it started to rise. As the warm water rose, it left a void, and that void was filled by cold water. The cold water got warmer, the warm water got cooler, and this created a convection current.

If you could see a cross-section of the sun, it would look a lot like the illustration below. The core of the sun is where the nuclear reaction, producing the energy of the sun, occurs. The temperature there is estimated to be 27 million degrees Fahrenheit. Next to the core is the radiative zone that is capped by a layer of supergranules.

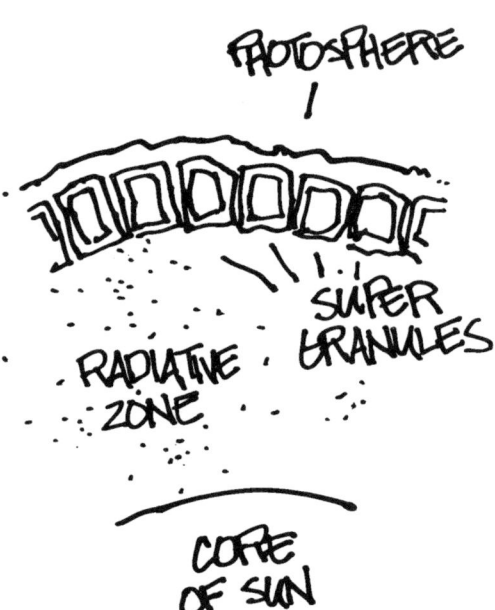

Supergranules are just like the convection tube that you have been using. They produce heated columns that rise to the surface of the sun, cool, and then descend back toward the radiative zone. Finally, there is the photosphere, which is the surface of the sun.

Science Fair Extensions

69. Find other containers that can be heated on one side, and set up a convection current.

70. Convection currents can also be established using hot and cold air. Create a replica of this experiment using air instead of water, with smoke as the indicator instead of food coloring. Be sure to get adult supervision.

3-D Magnetic Fields

The Experiment

Most of the time, folks see magnetic fields as flat, two-dimensional configurations, when in actuality, they are three-dimensional. The problem is that the way we look at magnets most of the time does not allow us to see all three dimensions. We are going to change that with this lab, which may also change your perception of how the magetic field that surrounds the sun appears.

We are going to incorporate a very strong magnet, called a cow magnet, used by cattle ranchers. Cow magnets are inserted into the first stomachs of range cattle. That way, when these silly animals eat barbed wire and old tin cans, the metal stays in the first stomach and does not pass through the system, causing bleeding.

Materials

1   Bottle of iron filings
1   16-oz. pop bottle, clear and clean
1   Cow magnet
1   Plastic test tube
1   Bicycle-tube section, 3 inches long
1   Rubberband

Procedure

1. Pop the lid off the iron-filing shaker and empty about half the bottle into the pop bottle that you have previously checked to make sure it is clean and dry.

2. Slide the cow magnet into the plastic test tube. Make sure that it slides all the way to the end.

3-D Magnetic Fields

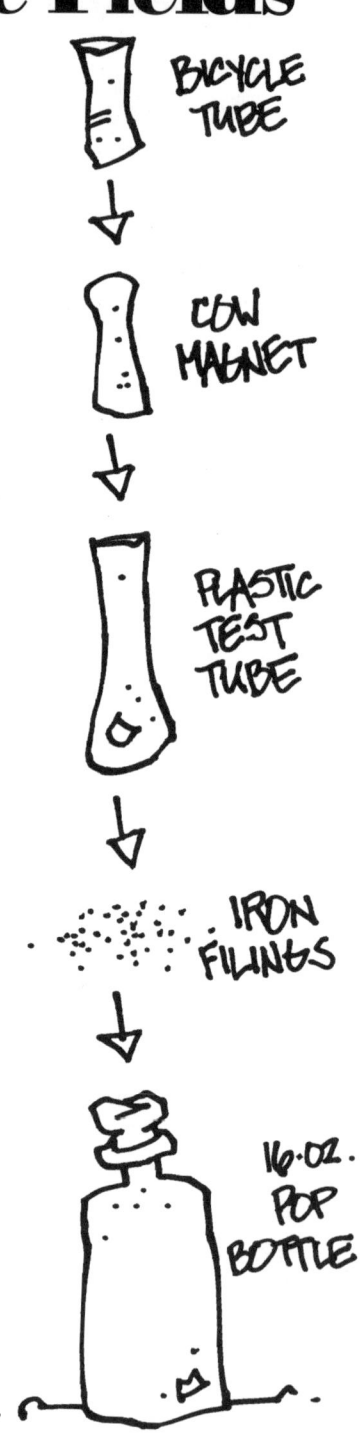

3. Place one end of the bicycle-tube section over the plastic test tube. Slide the tube inside the bottle and fold the other end of the bicycle tube over the mouth of the bottle. This will enclose the bottle and keep the iron filings from flying all over the place. Use the illustration at the right as a guide.

4. When you are ready, give the bottle a couple of good shakes. This will toss the iron filings up into the air, and they will come in contact with the magnetic field of the cow magnet. As the iron filings stick to the test tube, a three-dimensional picture of the magnetic field will appear. Pay special attention to the concentration of filings near the poles as well as to the orientation of the iron filings near the middle. You'll clearly see that the strength of the magnet is in its poles.

5. When it is time to clean up, simply lift the magnet gently toward the mouth of the bottle, and roll the bicycle-tube section back. When the magnet is completely out of the bicycle-tube section, the iron filings will fall back into the bottle.

How Come, Huh?

The cow magnet has a very strong magnetic field. As the iron filings are tossed around the inside of the bottle, they are attracted to the magnetic field that radiates out from the magnet. Because the filings are small and can be influenced to move in any direction, they align with the lines of force and create a three-dimensional picture of the magnetic field.

If you could sprinkle a giant shaker of iron filings and take a picture of the magnetic field around the sun, it would probably look something like the model that you have in your pop bottle.

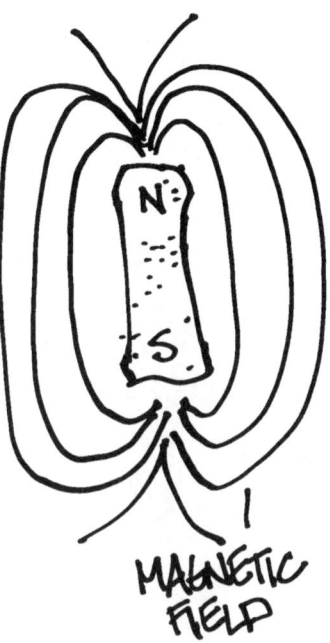

MAGNETIC FIELD

Science Fair Extensions

71. OK, a giant can of iron filings is a little bit impractical, to say the least. Astronomers measure the presence of a magnetic field using compasses that record and transmit information back to Earth. Demonstrate a way to use a compass to detect and draw the outline of the magnetic field of the cow magnet.

72. Mix up a batch of Jello with iron filings in it, and let it set up on top of a cow magnet. See if the pattern in the Jello reflects the pattern that was created in the bottle.

73. Find out what Ferrofluid is and how it is used to create 3-dimensional patterns.

Big Idea 6

Constellations are 2-dimensional groupings of stars that may be different ages and degrees of brightness, and often are millions of light years apart.

Galactic Cookie Dough • B. K. Hixson

Classifying Stars

The Experiment
The mass of a star not only dictates the life of the star and its eventual end but it also influences its other properties—color, temperature, and luminosity.

Materials
1   Box of colored pencils

Procedure
The Harvard System of Star Classification assigns a letter to each star based on the surface temperature of the star. Listed below are the colors associated with certain temperatures. Use that information to fill in the circles at the right, starting with the first color for the top circle, and continue down in the order that is listed.

Star Color	Surface Temp
Baby blue	90,000 ° F
Light blue	54,000 ° F
White	18,000 ° F
Yellow	10,800 ° F
Orange	7,200 ° F
Red-orange	6,300 ° F
Red	6,300 ° F

W   ○

O   ○

B   ○

A   ○

F   ○

G

K   ○

M   ○

Science Fair Extensions
74. Find out what an HR diagram is, where a particular star fits on that diagram, and just exactly what information that diagram will tell you.

Measuring Magnitude

The Experiment

The brightness (also called the magnitude) of a star is a function of two different factors, its luminosity (the amount of light energy produced) and its distance from the Earth. This magnitude is measured using two different scales. The first, absolute magnitude, compares all stars with one another from a standard distance. The second, apparent magnitude, describes how bright a star appears when viewed from Earth.

In this lab, you are to compare two stars, Rigel and Sirius, using both apparent and absolute magnitude readings. In the second part of the lab, you are going to construct a model that demonstrates the apparent magnitude of stars using a flashlight and layers of wax paper.

Materials

1   Pair of scissors
1   Flashlight w/new batteries
1   Pencil
1   Partner
1   Soup can
6   Sheets of wax paper
6   Pieces of cardboard, 6 inches by 6 inches each
1   Roll of masking tape
1   Dark room

Procedure

1. Using the scale located at the top of the *Data & Observations* section that compares the apparent and absolute magnitudes of stars side by side, plot the location of Rigel and Sirius using the numbers provided.

	Apparent Magnitude	Absolute Magnitude
Rigel	+ 0.12	- 7.1
Sirius	- 1.46	+ 1.4

2. After plotting the magnitudes of Rigel and Sirius, take the soup can and place it in the center of one of the sheets of cardboard. Trace the outline of the can. Do this with all six pieces of cardboard and then cut the circles from the cardboard so that there is a hole in each of the pieces.

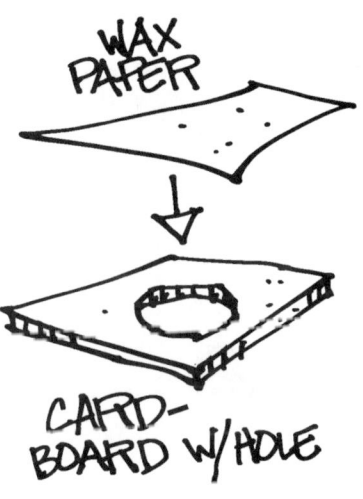

3. Cut five squares of wax paper that are 4 inches by 4 inches each. Place each piece of wax paper over the hole in the center each of the five cardboard squares and tape them in place. Use the illustration at the right as a guide.

4. Apparent star magnitude is a simple, straightforward observation of how bright the light of a star appears when you are standing on Earth. The scale runs from one to six, one being the brightest and six being very faint.

Measuring Magnitude

5. Darken the room. Place the first piece of cardboard, with no wax paper covering the hole, over the end of the flashlight. Ask your partner to turn the flashlight on and shine it toward you. Use the illustration at the bottom of the page as a guide to set this up. Note the brightness of the light and leave the first circle in the sequence on page 151 blank so it is very white and bright.

6. Leaving the first piece of cardboard in place, add a second piece so that the light is now shining through one piece of wax paper. Observe and draw the intensity of the light. This means that you will have to lightly shade the second circle to show that some of the light is filtered out by the atmosphere and distance.

7. Continue adding pieces of wax paper/cardboard and coloring in the squares until you have a pile of all six pieces of cardboard in front of the flashlight and the amount of light is very faint.

Data & Observations

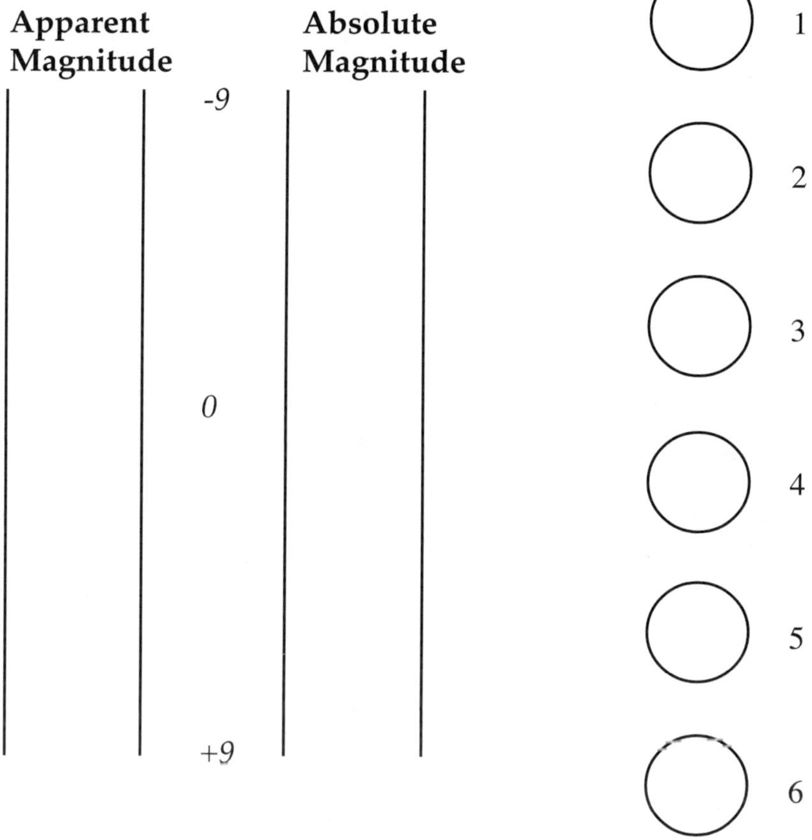

Apparent Magnitude	Absolute Magnitude
-9	
0	
+9	

○ 1

○ 2

○ 3

○ 4

○ 5

○ 6

How Come, Huh?

Sirius appears brighter than Rigel in the night sky, but the truth of the matter is that if you were to compare them side by side, Rigel would completely outshine Sirius. It's all perspective.

Science Fair Extensions

75. Find out what a red shift is, what it tells us, and how astronomers can detect it.

Hand-Held Black Holes

The Experiment
Two bottles are connected in the middle with a piece of plastic, called a Tornado Tube. The top bottle is full of water and the bottom is full of air. Tornados, black holes, vortexes, and the death of a massive star, all in one lab!

Materials
1   Tornado Tube
2   Pop bottles, 2 liters or 1 liter each
1   Clock with sweep-second hand
    Water

Procedure

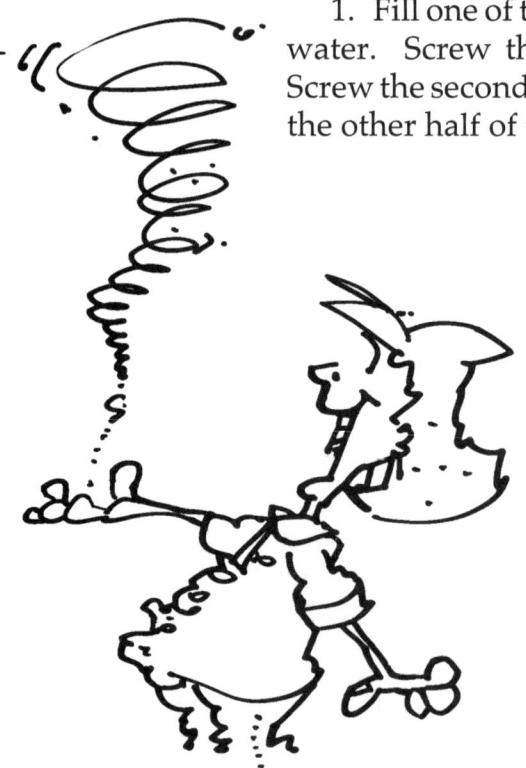

1. Fill one of the pop bottles two-thirds full with water. Screw the Tornado Tube onto the bottle. Screw the second pop bottle, which is full of air, into the other half of the Tornado Tube.

2. Flip the connection that you have just made upside down and record the amount of time that it takes for the water to move from the top bottle to the bottom one in the data table on the next page.

3. Flip it over again, grab the top bottle as is shown in the picture at the left, and make large circles with your upper hand until the water starts swirling in the shape of a vortex. Record the time it takes the water to empty into the bottom bottle again.

Data & Observations

Trial	Time to Empty
1	
2	

How Come, Huh?

When you turn the bottles over without spinning them (Trial #1), the water pretty much stays in the top bottle. That's because the air in the bottom bottle blocks the water in the top bottle. In order to get the water into the bottom bottle, you have to exchange it with air from the bottom bottle.

When you spin the bottles (Trial #2), you create a force that pushes the water to the outside. Water molecules tend to hang onto one another—a characteristic called cohesion. So, if you get water molecules going in a particular direction, they tend to drag their buddies along with them.

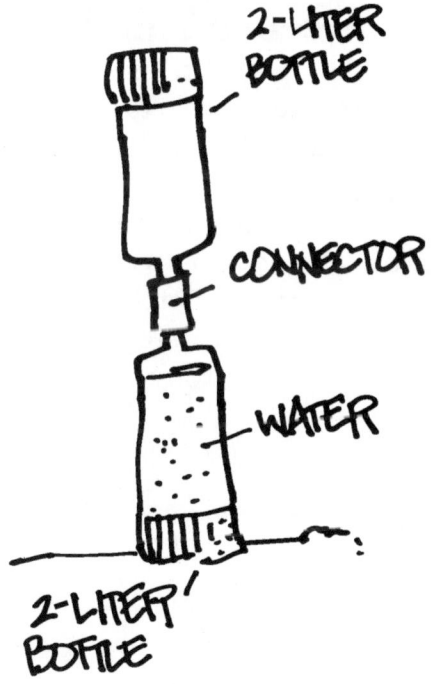

This leaves a gap in the center that the air can use to move from the bottom bottle to the top bottle. As this happens, water moves down the sides into the bottom bottle. The water continues spinning like a tornado because once something is in motion, it tends to stay in motion. If you want to impress friends and family, this is called rotational inertia.

Hand-Held Black Holes

When liquids are exposed to a circular force, they start to form a vortex, or tornado. The center of the tornado consists of empty space filled with air, and the sides of the tornado are composed of water molecules. One of the characteristics of a tornado is that air rushes up inside the vortex—along with small dogs, fenceposts, and old ladies on bicycles.

As far as astronomy goes, a black hole is the by-product of a massive star that has expired. When a massive star has consumed most of its helium, it becomes a red giant. The red giant eventually sheds its outer gas layers, and gravity causes the star to condense and then explode in what is called a supernova. After the explosion, all that is left is a very dense, dark, rotating mass that is so heavy that even light cannot escape its grasp—a black hole. Nothing evades a black hole's gravitational attraction.

Science Fair Extensions

76. Use different-sized pop bottles, and see if the size of the tornado is any different.

77. Prove that you can get the tornado to swirl clockwise and then counterclockwise. See if it is possible to reverse the flow halfway through the experiment.

Soup Can Constellation

The Experiment

Constellations are arbitrary groups of stars that form a pattern. Most people can look in the night sky and identify a collection of seven bright stars as The Big Dipper. To Native Americans, that same pattern of stars is a large bear. To other groups of people, it could represent something entirely different.

The truth is that even though they look like they may go together, most of the time the stars are incredible distances apart— sometimes hundreds of millions of miles apart. We make the associations down here on Earth. There are legends and explanations for these patterns, which are characteristic of almost every group of people from the ancient Greeks, Romans, and Mayans to the Native Americans and Eskimos of North America, and even to modern-day astrology. In this lab, you will have the opportunity to construct some known constellations and also dream up some of your own.

Materials

1   Empty soup can
1   Flashlight
1   Pen/pencil
7   Sheets of aluminum foil

Procedure

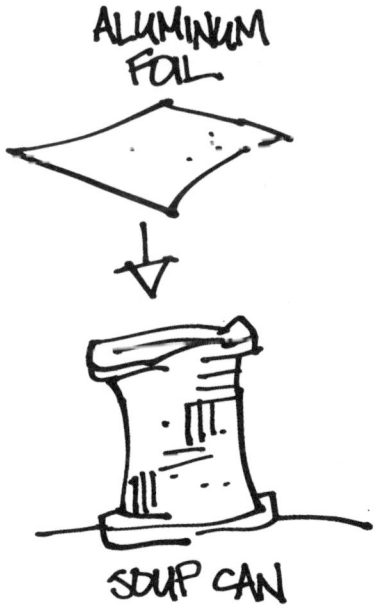

ALUMINUM FOIL

SOUP CAN

1. Make sure that both ends of the soup can have been removed and that the inside of the can is dry and clean. Take a single sheet of aluminum foil, wrap it over the end of your soup can, and hold it in place with a rubberband. Use the illustration at the right as a guide.

Soup Can Constellation

2. Once you have the aluminum foil in place, gently punch holes in it to form a constellation, as pictured in an encyclopedia or other reference book. When the constellation is complete, slide the flashlight into the can and either look directly at the pattern of dots that have been created or project the constellation on the wall.

3. Repeat the previous step with four other constellations and practice identifying them with your classmates. When you get to the point where you can identify each of the constellations by sight, use the remaining two sheets of aluminum foil to create your own constellations. Dream up a pattern and a story to go with them and then take turns sharing your creations with classmates.

Data & Observations

In the boxes provided below and on the next page, draw some of the constellations that you either copied or created from your imagination. Be sure to write the name of the constellation under each drawing. If it is constellation that you made up, write its name in capital letters; if it is one that you copied, write its name in small letters.

How Come, Huh?

This lab introduced you to the concept of constellations, or groupings of stars that humans have associated with shapes and folklore.

Science Fair Extensions

78. Research different constellations and find a way of depicting their shapes using common household items.

Mapping Orion

The Experiment

When we view constellations from the Earth, they appear to be two-dimensional collections of stars. The truth is that they are anything but two-dimensional. In this lab, you are going to map the main stars in the constellation Orion in three dimensions.

Materials

1   Pair of scissors
1   Index card, 3 inches by 5 inches
2   Sheets of corrugated cardboard, 8 inches by 11 inches
1   Hole punch
8   Pins with round heads
1   Metric ruler
    Tape

Procedure

1. Pictured below is the pattern for the constellation Orion. Copy it onto the index card.

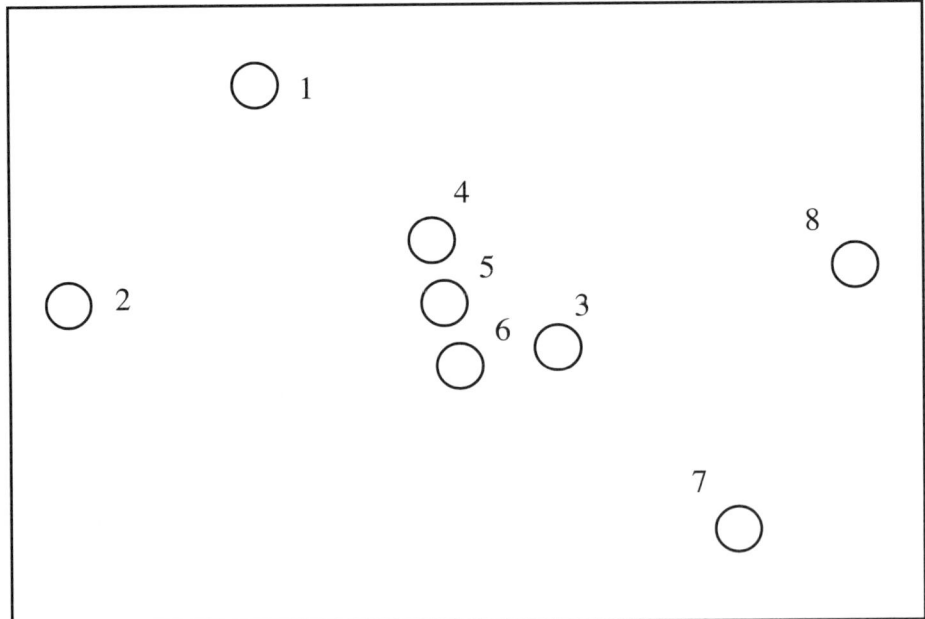

2. Using the hole punch, make a hole where each of the circles appears on the card.

3. Tape the card to the edge of a piece of corrugated cardboard, as shown in the picture below. Then, using your metric ruler, mark every centimeter from the edge of the card (where the constellation pattern is taped) to 30 cm. Make large lines all the way across the cardboard every 5 cm and short hash marks every 1 cm.

4. Now add a second piece of cardboard to the first one, but make the cardboard face the other way. Tape it to the first piece of cardboard so that you have a very long piece of cardboard. Measure 20 cm from the center edge of the two pieces of cardboard, make an "X," and write the word *Earth* under it. This will be your point of perspective for constructing the 3-D pattern of the constellation.

Mapping Orion

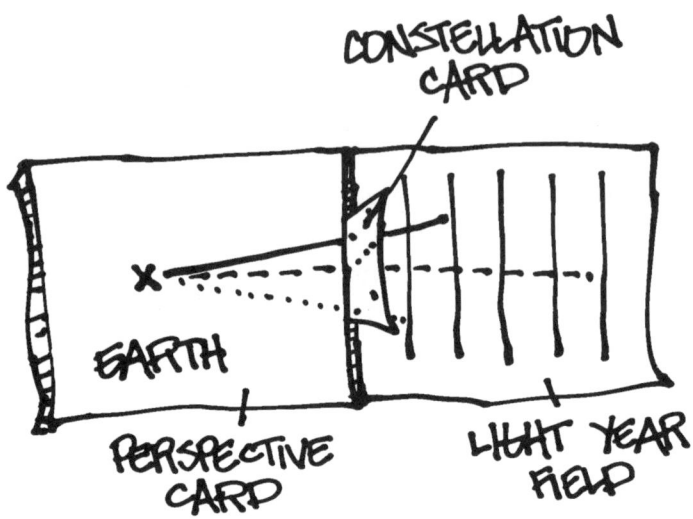

5. Place the edge of the ruler directly under the hole for Star #1. Align the ruler so that it passes through the "X." Draw a straight line connecting the card to the "X." Do this for all 8 holes so that you have a pattern that looks something like the illustration above.

6. Time to plot the first star. Locate Star #1 in the *Data & Observations* section. It is located 1,400 light years away from Earth. Each major line represents 500 light years, and the hash marks represent 100 light years.

Here's how you plot the position of Star #1. Locate the horizontal line for 1,400 light years. Position the ruler on the side of the card with the lines, and eyeball it so that it lines up with the Earth. Draw a line from the back of the constellation card out to the 1,400 light year line. Stick a pin at the point where the sight line with the Earth passes through the 1,400 light years line. This is the relative location of the star.

7. Continue on and plot the location of the other seven stars. When you are done, your card should look something like the illustration on the next page.

Data & Observations

Star	Light Years from Earth	Name
1	1,400	
2	900	Rigel
3	1,500	Orion Nebula
4	1,100	
5	1,200	
6	2,300	Mintaka
7	400	Betelgeuse
8	100	

Science Fair Extensions

79. Research the rest of the names for each of the eight stars in Orion's constellation.

Zodiac Hunter

The Experiment

The zodiac is a collection of 12 constellations that are crossed by the sun's ecliptic path (the sun's annual path around the celestial sphere) and form the backdrop for the moon and the planets. The sun spends approximately one month passing through each of the constellations and, over time, people have produced a number of stories, legends, and myths to go along with the sun's movement past the constellations.

Materials

1 Black umbrella
1 Jar of glow in the dark paint

Procedure

1. If you were to cover the sky with a giant umbrella, you would have a sense of what a three-dimensional replica of the hemisphere would look like. We are going to use that idea to create a star locator out of an old umbrella.

2. Locate a book that has a collection of pictures of the night sky. In it, find a representation of the 12 zodiac constellations. Divide the umbrella into 12 even sections and, using the pattern in the book, paint the constellations on the inside of the umbrella using the glow in the dark paint.

3. To use your constellation locator, wait until dark and head outside, preferably on a moonless night. Locate the North Star (Polaris) in the night sky and then locate the constellations of the zodiac that are visible.

Science Fair Extensions

80. Use the zodiac hunter to demonstrate how the constellations of the night sky change during the seasons. Also explain why some constellations are not always visible.

81. Make a complimentary zodiac hunter for the southern hemisphere. Determine which constellations stay the same and which ones differ from one side of the world to the other.

Big Idea 7

Rockets and space travel have captured our imaginations, even if our ideas behind the physics aren't quite correct.

Rocket on a String

The Experiment

Newton's Second Law: *A law of physics that we see in sporting events and NASCAR™ racing all the time.* The formula for the Law is written as *F=ma*, or, force equals mass times acceleration. In other words, the more energy you apply to an object, the faster and farther it will go. The maximum application of this law is the object of any shot-putter, most javelin throwers, and the average second grader standing on the bank of a river with a fistful of rocks.

Here, we are going to ex-
periment with balloon rockets.
These rockets will give you a better idea of what Newton's Second
Law is about.

Materials

2   Balloons
1   Straw
1   Piece of string, 30 feet long
4   Strips of masking tape,
      each 4 inches long
1   Partner

Procedure

1. You will be working with a partner through all of these steps. With your partner, thread the string through the straw.

2. Inflate a balloon, but do not tie it off. You will need the air to escape to provide the necessary thrust for your rocket. Using two pieces of masking tape, attach the balloon to the straw. Use the illustration on the next page as a guide.

Rocket on a String

3. Ask your partner to walk to the other end of the room with the string. You should have the balloon in one hand, pinching the neck to hold the air in, and the end of the string in the other. Your partner should hold the opposite end of the string.

4. When everyone is ready, the balloon holder needs to lift the balloon to chin level for launch and the partner needs to hold the other end of the string at belly-button level. You will say, "three, two, one, launch!," and when you come to the word, "launch," let go of your balloon, allowing the air to escape. This will push the balloon forward.

5. After you have completed your flight, work with your partner to fill in the data table on the next page. You will launch and record the amount of time it takes for your balloon to travel to the end of the string three times. Average those times and enter that information in the data table.

6. Add a second balloon and race the two "engines" down your string three more times. Once all of the data has been entered, create a *bar graph* on page 168 showing the information. After that is complete, *infer* how fast you think a rocket with three and four "engines" would travel by drawing bars to represent what you *think* the data would look like.

Galactic Cookie Dough • B. K. Hixson

Data & Observations

Rocket	Time Measurements		
	Trial #1 (sec.)	Trial #2 (sec.)	Trial #3 (sec.)
1 Balloon Engine			
2 Balloon Engines			

1 Balloon Engine   _____ (Average Time)

2 Balloon Engines   _____ (Average Time)

3 Balloon Engines   _____ (Inferred Time)

4 Balloon Engines   _____ (Inferred Time)

How Come, Huh?

As you released the neck of the balloon, air began escaping out the back—the action. For every action, there is an equal and opposite reaction. In this case, the air pushed against the front and sides of the balloon, producing a net forward force, and so the balloon propelled along the string. As you might have noticed, there is an illustration on the top of page 166 that was designed to give you a bit of visual insight into exactly what we are talking about.

Rocket on a String

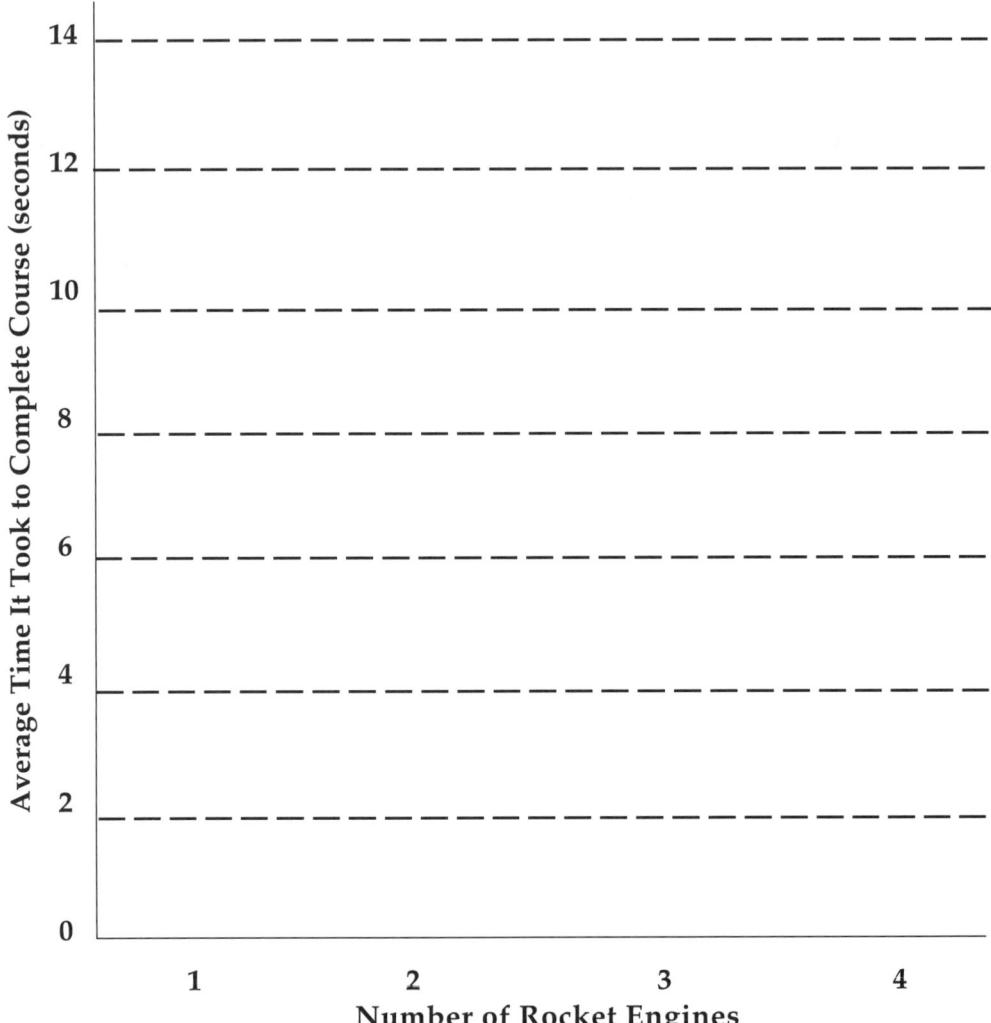

Science Fair Extensions

82. Change the track that the balloon rocket travels down by using different materials. Try twine, fishing line, steel wire, and so forth.

83. Determine if the shape of the engine— round vs. oblong— makes a difference in the speed at which a rocket travels.

84. See if your results replicate when going uphill at a 45-degree angle.

Portable Space Cannon

The Experiment

Is that an alien voice I hear? I don't think so. It's probably your lab partner creating some weird vibrations on a space cannon. This activity demonstrates sound but also emphasizes that you need matter in order to have sound. Do you think we could chat in outer space?

Materials

1   Metal Slinky
1   Pencil
1   1-gallon plastic milk jug, empty
1   Pair of scissors
1   Pair of clean ears
1   Roll of masking tape
1   Partner

Procedure

1. Using the scissors, cut off the top third of the plastic milk jug. Be sure to recycle it.

2. Using the point of the scissors, punch a very small opening in the bottom of the jug.

3. Thread one end of the Slinky through the hole in the bottom of the jug. Tape it inside.

4. Give the other end of the Slinky to your partner. Ask your partner to gently stretch the spring out and away from you and the gallon jug that you are holding.

Portable Space Cannon

5. Hold the open end of the milk jug up near your ear and ask your partner to whap the spring with a pencil. Stretch the spring out and listen to the sound that is produced. Walk toward each other and let the spring droop a bit. Listen to the sound.

6. After you have used the pencil, ask your partner to flick the spring with a fingernail. Listen to the quality of this new sound and try to describe it in the table below. Then have your partner whap the spring with the fleshy part of a finger. Record your new observations.

Data & Observations

Object	Sound Produced
Pencil	
Fingernail	
Finger	

How Come, Huh?

If we were in space, we wouldn't be able to hear one another. Why? No matter! In order for sound to travel, we have to have vibrations. If we are going to have vibrations, then we have to have something that will vibrate. That's where matter comes in. Different kinds of matter produce different kinds of sound waves.

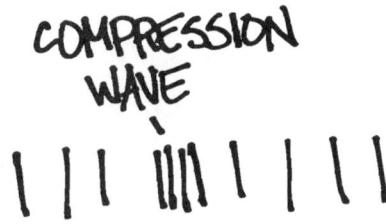

Metal objects transmit sound very, very quickly, through a matrix of metal atoms that are highly ordered and have a great deal of structure. When the sound wave that was produced by the pencil whapping the spring reaches the plastic milk jug, it is collected and amplified. The metallic nature of the sound becomes greater. That's what happens when you hear sounds like the "cannons" that are often used in space movies.

Science Fair Extensions

85. You can change lots of variables in this experiment. Try different sizes of and materials for a) Slinky toys, b) milk jugs, and c) items with which to whap the spring.

86. Make a space phone using the Slinky.

Sound Sponge

The Experiment

A sponge is an animal, or, in the case of modern production, it's a synthetic material that absorbs liquids. A sound sponge, it stands to reason, is a material that soaks up sound. It absorbs sound so that it cannot escape or be shared. This is precisely the point of this lab activity.

Sound can travel through solids, liquids, and gases, but it cannot travel through a vacuum. In a vacuum, there is nothing for the vibrating object to push on. There is no material to transfer the energy to. That is why space is a very quiet place ... unless you are thinking of the way it's depicted in the movies.

Materials

1   Vacuum pump
1   Bell jar with platform
1   Wind-up bell or buzzer

Procedure

1. Hook the vacuum pump up to the bell jar and make sure that the pump is properly evacuating air from inside.

2. Wind up a buzzer or bell and place it on the bell jar platform. Start the buzzer buzzing and place the bell jar over the buzzer. Because there is air inside the jar, you should be able to hear the buzzing sound produced by the vibrations.

3. Turn on the vacuum pump and start to remove air from inside the bell jar. Listen very carefully to the sound that is being made by the buzzer. You should notice that, as more and more air is removed from inside the jar, the sound is becoming quieter and quieter.

4. Continue to evacuate air until there is no more left inside the bell jar. At this point in time, the buzzer should still be vibrating away, but no audible sound should be transferred outside the bell jar.

5. Slowly release the stopcock on the vacuum pump, allowing air to seep back into the jar. As the amount of air increases, the volume of the buzzer should also increase.

How Come, Huh?

When there is no matter to push against or transfer energy to, no sound can be passed along from one molecule to another. By removing all of the air from inside the bell jar, you removed the matter that the buzzer was going to push against. If there is no matter, then there is no way for sound waves to form.

So, next time you are sitting back and watching your favorite SciFi space battle rage on, smile, enjoy the movie, and know that if you were there, all would be quiet.

Doppler Demo

The Experiment

All kids know the sound of a car passing in front of them on a racetrack … even if they've never been to the Indy-500. I would bet that 99% of your friends can make that sound, if you ask them. This is a racy way to learn about the Doppler Effect. You will use embroidery hoops or create your own paper loop sound waves to demonstrate how the idea works.

Pretend you have front-row seats at the Indy-500. Can you imitate the sound the cars make as they speed by in front of you? The pitch seems to go from high to low, but do you know why? When sound waves are bunched up in the front of a car, they create a high-frequency pitch. When they are spread out in the back of the car, they create a lower-frequency pitch. Using circles of various sizes, you can demonstrate this Doppler Effect.

Materials

5   Construction paper strips, 1 inch thick, 11 inches long
1   Pair of scissors
1   Small toy car
1   Bottle of glue

Procedure

1. The paper should be cut from a standard sheet of construction paper. We will assume that the longest piece is 11 inches long. Cut strips of 10 inches, 9 inches, 8 inches, and 7 inches.

2. Connect the ends of the paper strips, making loops out of each one. Then place the rings, one inside the other. Use the illustration shown here as a guide.

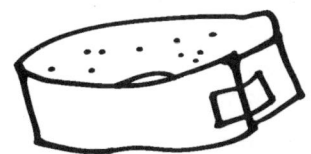

3. Place the small car in the center of the rings, and "drive" it to one side of the rings.

4. The rings should bunch up in front of the car and spread out in the back of the car. You have just created a visual model of what happens to sound waves as a car passes in front of you very quickly.

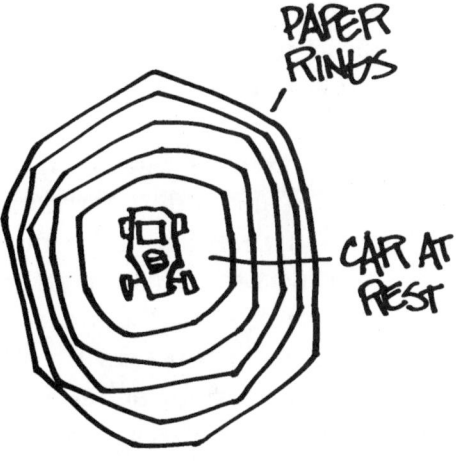

PAPER RINGS

CAR AT REST

How Come, Huh?

When a car is idling, sitting still with the engine running, the sound waves travel out in all directions equally, relative to the position of the car. That would be the first arrangement of rings (sound waves) and your car.

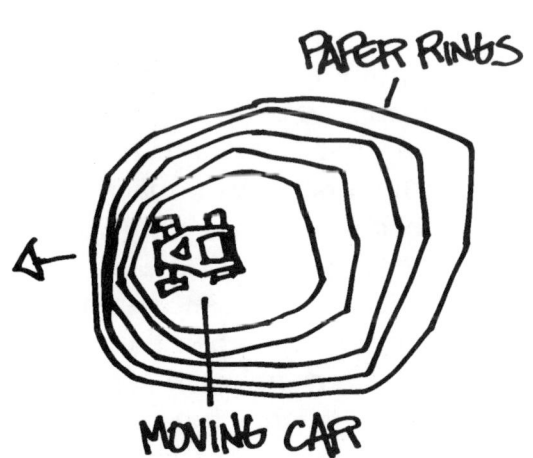

PAPER RINGS

MOVING CAR

Doppler Demo

As the car travels forward, it moves away from one edge of the first sound wave and toward the other. At the same time that the car is moving, it is also producing another sound wave. This second sound wave is not spaced equally, like when the car was idling. Instead, it is a little closer to one side and a little farther from the other.

The car moves again. It gets closer still to one side of the first sound, and farther from the other. When sound waves bunch up and get closer together, they produce a higher pitch. So, when a car traveling really fast comes toward you, the sound waves are bunched up, and they produce a high pitch.

After the car passes you, the waves are spreading out. The farther apart the waves are, the lower the pitch that is produced. That's where you get the Doppler Effect. The sound starts high because the waves are all scrunched together. When the vehicle passes, the waves spread out, and the pitch gets lower rapidly.

Enough Indy-500 stuff! How does all this apply to phenomena that affect the Earth and its atmosphere? Well, all we have to do to answer that question is focus on rain, winds, and even tornados, all of which have an impact on our planet. By focusing on these phenomena, we can see how useful our knowledge of the Doppler Effect really is.

The same ideas that apply to sound apply to rain when it is falling and winds when they shift. To collect data about both, the Doppler radar antenna is enlisted to pump out microwaves. The microwaves bounce into the falling raindrops and bounce back to the antenna. By comparing the rate with which the waves return to the antenna, we can determine whether a storm is moving away from the radar or toward it. In addition to that, by comparing winds in different areas and color-coding them, we can even detect a tornado up to 20 minutes before the funnel cloud hits the surface of the Earth.

Science Fair Extensions

87. Head outside and collect actual recordings of the Doppler Effect. Be sure to use caution if you are near a roadway where cars and trucks are traveling at high speeds. You may also want to go to the airport, where planes are taking off and landing. This is another excellent place to hear the Doppler Effect firsthand.

Instead of engine noises, collect siren sounds from police cars, ambulances, or fire stations.

Science Fair Projects
•
A Step-by-Step Guide: From Idea to Presentation

Galactic Cookie Dough • B. K. Hixson

Science Fair Projects

Ah, the impending science fair project—a good science fair project has the following five characteristics:

1. The student must come up with an *original* question.
2. That *original* question must be suited to an experiment in order to provide an answer.
3. The *original* idea is outlined with just one variable isolated.
4. The *original* experiment is performed and documented using the scientific method.
5. A presentation of the *original* idea in the form of a lab write-up and display board is completed.

Science Fair Projects

As simple as science report versus science fair project sounds, it gets screwed up millions of times a year by sweet, unsuspecting students who are counseled by sweet, unknowing, and probably just-as-confused parents.

To give you a sense of contrast, we have provided a list of legitimate science fair projects and then reports that do not qualify. We will also add some comments in italics that should help clarify why they do or do not qualify in the science fair project department.

Science Fair Projects

1. Temperature and the amount of time it takes mealworms to change to beetles.

Great start. We have chosen a single variable that is easy to measure: temperature. From this point forward, the student can read, explore, and formulate an original question that is the foundation for the project.

A colleague of mine actually did a similar type of experiment for his master's degree. His topic: The rate of development of fly larvae in cow poop as a function of temperature. No kidding. He found out that the warmer the temperature of the poop, the faster the larvae developed into flies.

2. The effect of different concentrations of soapy water on seed germination.

Again, wonderful. Measuring the concentration of soapy water. This leads naturally into original questions and a good project.

3. Crystal size and the amount of sugar in the solution.

This could lead into other factors, such as exploring the temperature of the solution, the size of the solution container, and other variables that may affect crystal growth. Opens a lot of doors.

vs. Science Reports

4. Helicopter rotor size and the speed at which the 'copter falls.

Size also means surface area, which is very easy to measure. The student who did this not only found the mathematical threshold with relationship to air friction, but she also had a ton of fun.

5. The ideal ratio of baking soda to vinegar to make a fire extinguisher.

Another great start. Easy to measure and track, and leads to a logical question that can either be supported or refuted with the data.

Each of these topics *measures* one thing, such as the amount of sugar, the concentration of soapy water, or the ideal size. If you start with an idea that allows you to mea-

sure something, then you can change it, ask questions, explore, and ultimately make a *prediction*, also called a *hypothesis*, and experiment to find out if you are correct. On the other hand, here are some well-meaning but misguided entries:

Science Reports, <u>not Projects</u>
1. Dinosaurs!

OK, great. Everyone loves dinosaurs, but where is the experiment? Did you find a new dinosaur? Is Jurassic Park alive and well, and are we headed there to breed, drug, or in some way test them? Probably not. This was a report on T. rex. Cool, but not a science fair project. And judging by the protest that this kid's mom put up when the kid didn't get his usual "A," it is a safe bet that she put a lot of time in and shared in the disappointment.

More Reports &

2. Our Friend the Sun

Another very large topic, no pun intended. This could be a great topic. Sunlight is fascinating. It can be split, polarized, reflected, refracted, measured, collected, and converted. However, this poor kid simply chose to write about the size of the sun, regurgitating facts about its features, cycles, and other astrofacts while simultaneously offending the American Melanoma Survivors Society. Just kidding about that last part.

3. Smokers' Poll

A lot of folks think that they are headed in the right direction here. Again, it depends on how the kid attacks the idea. Are they going to single out race? Heredity? Shoe size? What exactly are they after here? The young lady who did this report chose to make it more of a psychology-studies effort than a scientific report. She wanted to know family income, if smokers fought with their parents, how much stress was on the job, and so on. All legitimate concerns, but not placed in the right slot.

4. The Majestic Moose

If you went out and caught the moose, drugged it to see the side effects for disease control, or even mated it with an elk to determine if you could create an animal that would become the spokesanimal for the Alabama Dairy Farmers' Got Melk? promotion, that would be fine. But, another fact-filled report should be filed with the English teacher.

5. How Tadpoles Change into Frogs

Great start, but they forgot to finish the statement. We know how tadpoles change into frogs. What we don't know is how tadpoles change into frogs if they are in an altered environment, if they are hatched out of cycle, or if they are stuck under the tire of an off-road vehicle blatantly driving through a protected wetland area. That's what we want to know—how tadpoles change into frogs, if, when, or under what measurable circumstances.

Now that we have beaten the chicken squat out of this introduction, we are going to show you how to pick a topic that can be adapted to become a successful science fair project after one more thought.

One Final Comment

A Gentle Reminder

Quite often I discuss the scientific method with moms and dads, teachers and kids, and get the impression that, according to their understanding, there is one, and only one, scientific method. This is not necessarily true. There are lots of ways to investigate the world we live in and on.

Paleontologists dig up dead animals and plants but have no way to conduct experiments on them. They're dead. Albert Einstein, the most famous scientist of the last century and probably on everybody's starting five of all time, never did experiments. He was a theoretical physicist, which means that he came up with a hypothesis, skipped over collecting materials for things like black holes and space-time continuums, and didn't experiment on anything or even collect data. He just went straight from hypothesis to conclusion, and he's still considered part of the scientific community. You'll probably follow the six steps we outline, but keep an open mind.

Project Planner

This outline is designed to give you a specific set of timelines to follow as you develop your science fair project. Most teachers will give you 8 to 11 weeks notice for this kind of assignment. We are going to operate from the shorter timeline with our suggested schedule, which means that the first thing you need to do is get a calendar.

A. The suggested time to be devoted to each item is listed in parentheses next to that item. Enter the date of the Science Fair and then, using the calendar, work backward entering dates.

B. As you complete each item, enter the date that you completed it in the column between the goal (due date) and project item.

Goal   Completed   Project Item

1. Generate a Hypothesis (2 weeks)

Goal	Completed	Project Item
_____	_____	Review Idea Section, pp. 188–189
_____	_____	Try Several Experiments
_____	_____	Hypothesis Generated
_____	_____	Finished Hypothesis Submitted
_____	_____	Hypothesis Approved

2. Gather Background Information (1 week)

Goal	Completed	Project Item
_____	_____	Concepts/Discoveries Written Up
_____	_____	Vocabulary/Glossary Completed
_____	_____	Famous Scientists in Field

& Timeline

Goal   Completed   *Project Item*

3. Design an Experiment (1 week)

————   ————   Procedure Written
————   ————   Lab Safety Review Completed
————   ————   Procedure Approved
————   ————   Data Tables Prepared
————   ————   Materials List Completed
————   ————   Materials Acquired

4. Perform the Experiment (2 weeks)

————   ————   Scheduled Lab Time

5. Collect and Record Experimental Data (part of 4)

————   ————   Data Tables Completed
————   ————   Graphs Completed
————   ————   Other Data Collected and Prepared

6. Present Your Findings (2 weeks)

————   ————   Rough Draft of Paper Completed
————   ————   Proofreading Completed
————   ————   Final Report Completed
————   ————   Display Completed
————   ————   Oral Report Outlined on Index Cards
————   ————   Practice Presentation of Oral Report
————   ————   Oral Report Presentation
————   ————   Science Fair Setup
————   ————   Show Time!

Scientific Method
• Step 1 •
The Hypothesis

Galactic Cookie Dough • B. K. Hixson

The Hypothesis

A hypothesis is an edu-cated guess. It is a statement of what you think will probably happen. It is also the most im-portant part of your science fair project because it directs the en-tire process. It determines what you study, the materials you will need, and how the experiment will be designed, carried out, and evaluated. Needless to say, you need to put some thought into this part.

There are four steps to generating a hypothesis:

Step One • Pick a Topic
Preferably something that you are interested in study-ing. We would like to politely recommend that you take a peek at physical science ideas (physics and chemistry) if you are a rookie and this is one of your first shots at a science fair project. These kinds of lab ideas allow you to repeat experiments quickly. There is a lot of data that can be collected, and there is a huge variety to choose from.

If you are having trouble finding an idea, all you have to do is pick up a compilation of science activities (like this one) and start thumbing through it. Go to the local library or head to a bookstore and you will find a wide and ever-changing selection to choose from. Find a topic that interests you and start reading. At some point, an idea will catch your eye, and you will be off to the races.

Pick a Topic . . .

We hope you find an idea you like between the covers of this book. But we also realize that 1) there are more ideas about astronomy than we have included in this book and 2) other kinds of presentations, or methods of writing labs, may be just what you need to trigger a new idea or put a different spin on things. So, without further ado, we introduce you to several additional titles that may be of help to you in developing a science fair project.

1. *Backpack Books 1001 Facts About Space* Written by Carole Stott and Clint Twist. ISBN 0-7894-8450-1. Published by Dorling Kindersley Ltd. 192 pages.

This easy-carry book on all kinds of facts about space was written by the experts, and it fits neatly in your backpack to carry nearly everywhere you want to look at the night sky. It starts with the universe, and pours out fact after fact, all the way down to how you see the stars from where you stand. And don't let its small size fool you: This little book has got a gigantic store of knowledge for you.

2. *Constellations for Every Kid* Written by Janice VanCleave. ISBN 0-471-15979-4. Published by John Wiley & Sons, Inc. 247 pages.

Our good friend Janice is going to take you on a tour of the stars, teaching you how to find all the constellations in the sky and where the names of all those patterns came from. Look up at the night sky, and, with this book and a trusty flashlight in hand, you'll be the brainiac of all the lore of the cosmos.

3. *Astronomy for Every Kid* Written by Janice VanCleave. ISBN 0-471-53573-7. Published by John Wiley & Sons, Inc. 229 pages.

A former science school teacher and presenter at museums and schools, Janice VanCleave has written educational books on many topics for kids. This book introduces you to the basics of astronomy, using simple experiments with an edge of fun that just won't quit.

Find an Idea You Like

4. *Astronomy Projects* Written by Issac Asimov. ISBN 0-8368-1229-8. Published by Gareth Stevens Publishing. 32 pages.

This great writer has produced a large work of astronomy books, from scientific in nature to fantastic fiction. This book serves as an introduction to astronomy by illustrating some basic principles of the universe, employing simple and inexpensive projects that you can perform in your own house.

5. *Science Fair Projects — Flight, Space & Astronomy* Written by Bob Bonnet & Dan Keen. ISBN 0-8069-9450-9. Published by Sterling Publishing Co., Inc. 95 pages.

Dreaming of being a scientist or an astronaut is a great ambition. Now you can get on the high road to success with this book! It will give you the basics of the worlds over our heads and make them simple to understand by giving you examples and experiments. Once you're done with this book, you'll be getting your science fair ribbons in no time. But why stop there? This book will get you ready to win the Nobel prize when you grow up!

6. *Space Encyclopedia* Written by Heather Couper and Nigel Henbest. ISBN 0-7894-4708-8. Published by DK Publishing, Inc. 304 pages.

If you're gonna be walking through the stars when you grow up, you'd better know your terminology before you go. This book will fill you in on all the lingo of space, from *Analyzing Light* to *X-Ray Astronomy*, the contents of this book provide a terrific basis for a well-founded knowledge of what happens in the way-up-yonder!

Develop an Original Idea

Step Two • Do the Lab

Choose a lab activity that looks interesting and try the experiment. Some kids make the mistake of thinking that all you have to do is find a lab in a book, repeat the lab, and you are on the gravy train with biscuit wheels. Your goal is to ask an ORIGINAL question, not repeat an experiment that has been done a bazillion times before.

As you do the lab, be thinking not only about the data you are collecting, but of ways you could adapt or change the experiment to find out new information. The point of the science fair project is to have you become an actual scientist and contribute a little bit of new knowledge to the world.

You know that they don't pay all of those engineers good money to sit around and repeat other people's lab work. The company wants new ideas so if you are able to generate and explore new ideas, you become very valuable, not only to that company but to society. It is the question-askers that find cures for diseases, create new materials, figure out ways to make existing machines energy-efficient, and change the way that we live. For the purpose of illustration, we are going to take a lab titled, "Prisms, Water Prisms" from another book, *Photon U*, and run it through the rest of the process. The lab uses a tub of water, an ordinary mirror, and light to create a prism that splits the light into the spectrum of a rainbow. Cool. Easy to do. Not expensive and open to all kinds of adaptations, including the four that we discuss on the next page.

Galactic Cookie Dough • B. K. Hixson

Step Three • Bend, Fold, Spindle, & Mutilate Your Lab

Once you have picked out an experiment, ask if it is possible to do any of the following things to modify it into an original experiment. You want to try and change the experiment to make it more interesting and find out one new, small piece of information.

Heat it	Freeze it	Reverse it	Double it
Bend it	Invert it	Poison it	Dehydrate it
Drown it	Stretch it	Fold it	Ignite it
Split it	Irradiate it	Oxidize it	Reduce it
Chill it	Speed it up	Color it	Grease it
Expand it	Substitute it	Remove it	Slow it down

If you take a look at our examples, that's exactly what we did to the main idea. We took the list of 24 different things that you could do to an experiment—not nearly all of them, by the way—and tried a couple of them out on the prism setup.

Double it: Get a second prism and see if you can continue to separate the colors further by lining up a second prism in the rainbow of the first.

Reduce it: Figure out a way to gather up the colors that have been produced and mix them back together to produce white light again.

Reverse it: Experiment with moving the flashlight and paper closer to the mirror and farther away. Draw a picture and be able to predict what happens to the size and clarity of the rainbow image.

Substitute it: You can also create a rainbow on a sunny day using a garden hose with a fine-spray nozzle attached. Set the nozzle adjustment so that a fine mist is produced and move the mist around in the sunshine until you see the rainbow. This works better if the sun is lower in the sky; late afternoon is best.

Hypothesis Worksheet

Step Three (Expanded) • Bend, Fold, Spindle Worksheet

This worksheet will give you an opportunity to work through the process of creating an original idea.

A. Write down the lab idea that you want to mangle.

_____

_____

_____

_____

B. List the possible variables you could change in the lab.

i. _____

ii. _____

iii. _____

iv. _____

v. _____

C'MON.
HE SAID TO
STRETCH IT.

C. Take one variable listed in section B and apply one of the 24 changes listed below to it. Write that change down and state your new lab idea in the space below. Do that with three more changes.

Heat it	Freeze it	Reverse it	Double it
Bend it	Invert it	Poison it	Dehydrate it
Drown it	Stretch it	Fold it	Ignite it
Split it	Irradiate it	Oxidize it	Reduce it
Chill it	Speed it up	Color it	Grease it
Expand it	Substitute it	Remove it	Slow it down

i. _____

_____

_____

Galactic Cookie Dough • B. K. Hixson

ii. _____

_____

_____

_____

iii. _____

_____

_____

_____

iv. _____

STRETCHING!

_____

_____

_____

Step Four • Create an Original Idea—Your Hypothesis
Your hypothesis should be stated as an opinion. You've done
the basic experiment, you've made observations, you're not stupid.
Put two and two together and make a PREDICTION. Be sure that you
are experimenting with just a single variable.

A. State your hypothesis in the space below. List the variable.
i. _____

_____

_____

_____

ii. Variable Tested: _____

Sample Hypothesis Worksheet

On the previous two pages is a worksheet that will help you develop your thoughts and a hypothesis. Here is sample of the finished product to help you understand how to use it.

A. Write down the lab idea that you want to mutilate.
A mirror is placed in a tub of water. A beam of light is focused through the water onto the mirror, producing a rainbow on the wall.

B. List the possible variables you could change in the lab.
      i. **Source of light**
      ii. **The liquid in the tub**
      iii. **The distance from flashlight to mirror**

C. Take one variable listed in section B and apply one of the 24 changes to it. Write that change down and state your new lab idea in the space below.

The shape of the beam of light can be controlled by making and placing cardboard filters over the end of the flashlight. Various shapes, such as circles, squares, and slits will produce different quality rainbows.

D. State your hypothesis in the space below. List the variable. Be sure that when you write the hypothesis, you are stating an idea and <u>not asking a question.</u>

Hypothesis: The narrower the beam of light, the tighter, brighter, and more focused the reflected rainbow will appear.

Variable Tested: The opening on the filter.

Scientific Method
• Step 2 •
Gather Information

Gather Information

Read about your topic and find out what we already know. Check books, videos, the Internet, and movies, talk with experts in the field, and molest an encyclopedia or two. Gather as much information as you can before you begin planning your experiment.

In particular, there are several things that you will want to pay special attention to and that should accompany any good science fair project.

A. Major Scientific Concepts
Be sure that you research and explain the main idea(s) that is / are driving your experiment. It may be a law of physics or chemical rule or an explanation of an aspect of plant physiology.

B. Scientific Words
As you use scientific terms in your paper, you should also define them in the margins of the paper or in a glossary at the end of the report. You cannot assume that everyone knows about geothermal energy transmutation in sulfur-loving bacteria. Be prepared to define some new terms for them ... and scrub your hands really well when you are done if that is your project.

C. Historical Perspective
When did we first learn about this idea, and who is responsible for getting us this far? You need to give a historical perspective with names, dates, countries, awards, and other recognition.

Building a Research Foundation

1. This sheet is designed to help you organize your thoughts and give you some ideas on where to look for information on your topic. When you prepare your lab report, you will want to include the background information outlined below.

    A. *Major Scientific Concepts (Two is plenty.)*
        i. _____

_____

_____

_____

        ii. _____

_____

_____

_____

    B. *Scientific Words (No more than 10)*
        i. _____
        ii. _____
        iii. _____
        iv. _____
        v. _____
        vi. _____
        vii. _____
        viii. _____
        ix. _____
        x. _____

    C. *Historical Perspective*
        Add this as you find it.

2. There are several sources of information that are available to help you fill in the details from the previous page.

A. *Contemporary Print Resources*
   (Magazines, Newspapers, Journals)

   i. _____

   ii. _____

   iii. _____

   iv. _____

   v. _____

   vi. _____

B. *Other Print Resources*
   (Books, Encyclopedias, Dictionaries, Textbooks)

   i. _____

   ii. _____

   iii. _____

   iv. _____

   v. _____

   vi. _____

C. *Celluloid Resources*
   (Films, Filmstrips, Videos)

   i. _____

   ii. _____

   iii. _____

   iv. _____

   v. _____

   vi. _____

D. Electronic Resources
(Internet Website Addresses, DVDs, MP3s)

i. _____

ii. _____

iii. _____

iv. _____

v. _____

vi. _____

vii. _____

viii. _____

ix. _____

x. _____

E. Human Resources
(Scientists, Engineers, Professionals, Professors, Teachers)

i. _____

ii. _____

iii. _____

iv. _____

v. _____

vi. _____

You may want to keep a record of all of your research and add it to the back of the report as an Appendix. Some teachers who are into volume think this is really cool. Others, like myself, find it a pain in the tuchus. No matter what you do, be sure to keep an accurate record of where you find data. If you quote from a report word for word, be sure to give proper credit with either a footnote or parenthetical reference. This is very important for credibility and accuracy. This will keep you out of trouble with plagiarism (copying without giving credit).

Scientific Method
• Step 3 •
Design Your Experiment

Galactic Cookie Dough • B. K. Hixson

Acquire Your Lab Materials

The purpose of this section is to help you plan your experiment. You'll make a map of where you are going, how you want to get there, and what you will take along.

List the materials you will need to complete your experiment in the table below. Be sure to list multiples if you will need more than one item. Many science materials double as household items in their spare time. Check around the house before you buy anything from a science supply company or hardware store. For your convenience, we have listed some suppliers on page 19 of this book.

	Material	Qty.	Source	$
1.				
2.				
3.				
4.				
5.				
6.				
7.				
8.				
9.				
10.				
11.				
12.				

Total $_____

Outline Your Experiment

This sheet is designed to help you outline your experiment. If you need more space, make a copy of this page to finish your outline. When you are done with this sheet, review it with an adult, make any necessary changes, review safety concerns on the next page, prepare your data tables, gather your equipment, and start to experiment.

In the space below, list what you are going to do in the order you are going to do it.

i. _____

_____

_____

ii. _____

_____

_____

iii. _____

_____

_____

iv. _____

_____

_____

v. _____

_____

_____

Evaluate Safety Concerns

We have included an overall safety section in the front of this book on pages 16-18, but there are some very specific questions you need to ask and prepare for, depending on the needs of your experiment. If you find that you need to prepare for any of these safety concerns, place a check mark next to the letter.

_____ *A. Goggles & Eyewash Station*
If you are mixing chemicals or working with materials that might splinter or produce flying objects, goggles and an eyewash station or sink with running water should be available.

_____ *B. Ventilation*
If you are mixing chemicals that could produce fire, smoke, fumes, or obnoxious odors, you will need to use a vented hood or go outside and perform the experiment in the fresh air.

_____ *C. Fire Blanket or Fire Extinguisher*
If you are working with potentially combustible chemicals or electricity, a fire blanket and extinguisher nearby are a must.

_____ *D. Chemical Disposal*
If your experiment produces a poisonous chemical or there are chemical-filled tissues (as in dissected animals), you may need to make arrangements to dispose of the by-products from your lab.

_____ *E. Electricity*
If you are working with materials and developing an idea that uses electricity, make sure that the wires are in good repair, that the electrical demand does not exceed the capacity of the supply, and that your work area is grounded.

_____ *F. Emergency Phone Numbers*
Look up and record the following phone numbers for the Fire Department: _____ , Poison Control: _____ , and Hospital: _____. Post them in an easy-to-find location.

Prepare Data Tables

Finally, you will want to prepare your data tables and have them ready to go before you start your experiment. Each data table should be easy to understand and easy for you to use.

A good data table has a **title** that describes the information being collected, and it identifies the **variable** and the **unit** being collected on each data line. The variable is *what* you are measuring and the unit is *how* you are measuring it. They are usually written like this:

Variable (unit), or to give you some examples:

Time (seconds)
Distance (meters)
Electricity (volts)

An example of a well-prepared data table looks like the sample below. We've cut the data table into thirds because the book is too small to display the whole line.

Determining the Boiling Point of Compound X_1

Time (min.)	0	1	2	3	4	5	6
Temp. (°C)							

Time (min.)	7	8	9	10	11	12	13
Temp. (°C)							

Time (min.)	14	15	16	17	18	19	20
Temp. (°C)							

Galactic Cookie Dough • B. K. Hixson

Scientific Method
• Step 4 •
Conduct the Experiment

Lab Time

It's time to get going. You've generated a hypothesis, collected the materials, written out the procedure, checked the safety issues, and prepared your data tables. Fire it up. Here's the short list of things to remember as you experiment.

_____ *A. Follow the Procedure and Record Any Changes*
Follow your own directions specifically as you wrote them. If you find the need to change the procedure once you are into the experiment that's fine; it's part of the process. Be sure to keep detailed records of the changes. When you repeat the experiment a second or third time, follow the new directions exactly.

_____ *B. Observe Safety Rules*
It's easier to complete the lab activity if you are in the lab rather than the emergency room.

_____ *C. Record Data Immediately*
Collect temperatures, distances, voltages, revolutions, and any other variables, and immediately record them into your data table. Do not think you will be able to remember them and fill everything in after the lab is completed.

_____ *D. Repeat the Experiment Several Times*
The more data that you collect, the better. It will give you a larger database and your averages will be more meaningful. As you do multiple experiments, be sure to identify each data set by date and time so you can separate them out.

_____ *E. Prepare for Extended Experiments*
Some experiments require days or weeks to complete, particularly those with plants and animals or the growing of crystals. Prepare a safe place for your materials so your experiment can continue undisturbed while you collect the data. Be sure you've allowed enough time for your due date.

Galactic Cookie Dough • *B. K. Hixson*

Scientific Method
• Step 5 •
Collect and Display Data

Types of Graphs

This section will give you some ideas on how you can display the information you are going to collect as a graph. A graph is simply a picture of the data that you gathered portrayed in a manner that is quick and easy to reference. There are four kinds of graphs described on the next two pages. If you find you need a leg up in the graphing department, we have a book in the series that will guide you through the process.

Line and Bar Graphs

These are the most common kinds of graphs. The most consistent variable is plotted on the "x," or horizontal, axis and the more temperamental variable is plotted along the "y," or vertical, axis. Each data point on a line graph is recorded as a dot on the graph, and then all of the dots are connected to form a picture of the data. A bar graph starts on the horizontal axis and moves up to the data line.

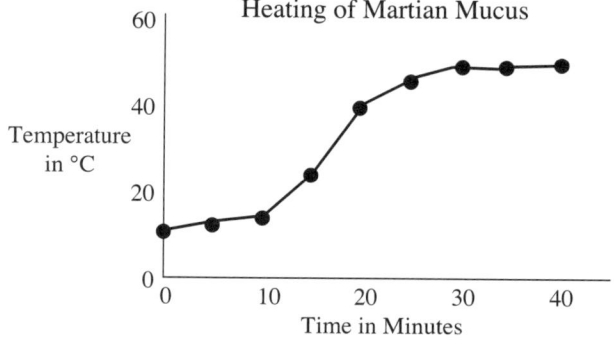

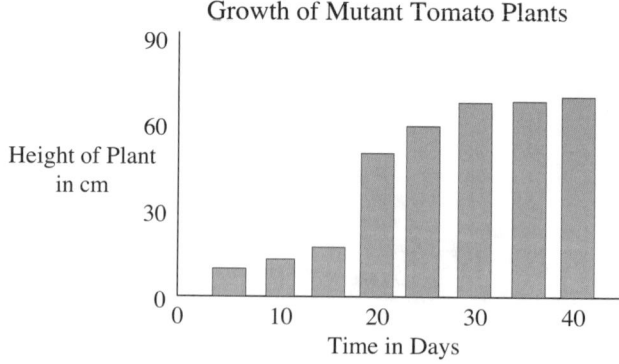

Best Fit Graphs

A best fit graph was created to show averages or trends rather than specific data points. The data that has been collected is plotted on a graph just as on a line graph, but instead of drawing a line from point to point to point, which sometimes is impossible anyway, you just freehand a line that hits "most of the data."

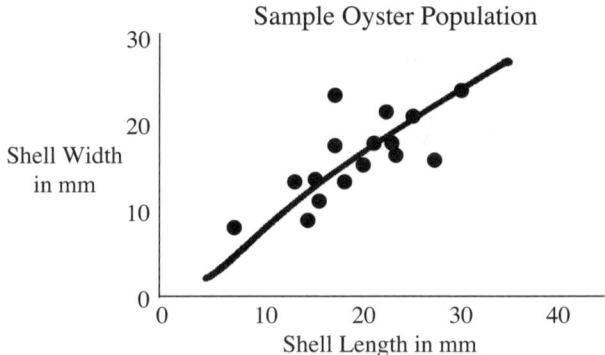

Pie Graphs

Pie graphs are used to show relationships between different groups. All of the data is totaled up and a percentage is determined for each group. The pie is then divided to show the relationship between one group and another.

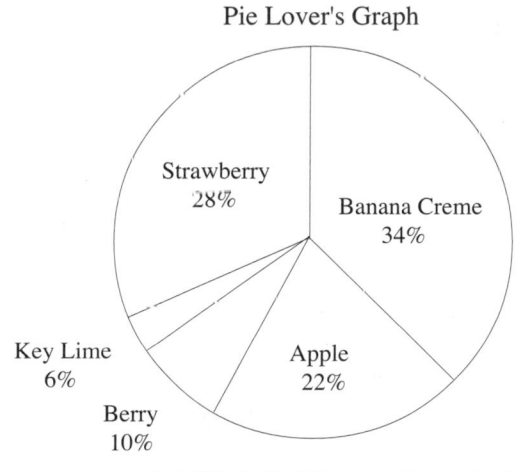

Other Kinds of Data

1. Written Notes & Observations

This is the age-old technique used by all scientists. Record your observations in a lab book. Written notes can be made quickly as the experiment is proceeding, and they can then be expounded upon later. Quite often, notes made in the heat of an experiment are revisited during the evaluation portion of the process, and they can shed valuable light on how or why the experiment went the way it did.

2. Drawings

Quick sketches as well as fully developed drawings can be used as a way to report data for a science experiment. Be sure to title each drawing and, if possible, label what it is that you are looking at. Drawings that are actual size are best.

3. Photographs, Videotapes, and Audiotapes

Usually better than drawings, quicker, and more accurate, but you do have the added expense and time of developing the film. However, they can often capture images and details that are not usually seen by the naked eye.

4. The Experiment Itself

Some of the best data you can collect and present is the actual experiment itself. Nothing will speak more effectively for you than the plants you grew, the specimens you collected, or that big pile of tissue that was an armadillo you peeled from the tread of an 18-wheeler.

Scientific Method
• Step 6 •
Present Your Ideas

Oral Report Checklist

It is entirely possible that you will be asked to make an oral presentation to your classmates. This will give you an opportunity to explain what you did and how you did it. Quite often, this presentation is part of your overall score, so if you do well, it will enhance your chances for one of the bigger awards.

To prepare for your oral report, your science fair presentation should include the following components:

Physical Display
- _____ a.   freestanding display board
    - hypothesis
    - data tables, graphs, photos, etc.
    - abstract (short summary)
- _____ b.   actual lab setup (equipment)

Oral Report
- _____ a.   hypothesis or question
- _____ b.   background information
    - concepts
    - word definitions
    - history or scientists
- _____ c.   experimental procedure
- _____ d.   data collected
    - data tables
    - graphs
    - photos or drawings
- _____ e.   conclusions and findings
- _____ f.   ask for questions

Set the display board up next to you on the table. Transfer the essential information to index cards. Use the index cards for reference, but do not read from them. Speak in a clear voice, hold your head up, and make eye contact with your peers. Ask if there are any questions before you finish and sit down.

Written Report Checklist

Next up is the written report, also called your lab write-up. After you compile or sort the data you have collected during the experiment and evaluate the results, you will be able to come to a conclusion about your hypothesis. Remember, disproving an idea is as valuable as proving it.

This sheet is designed to help you write up your science fair project and present your data in an organized manner. This is a final checklist for you.

To prepare your write-up, your science fair report should include the following components:

_____	a.	binder
_____	b.	cover page, title, & your name
_____	c.	abstract (one paragraph summary)
_____	d.	table of contents with page numbers
_____	e.	hypothesis or question
_____	f.	background information

> concepts
> word definitions
> history or scientists

_____	g.	list of materials used
_____	h.	experimental procedure

> written description
> photo or drawing of setup

_____	i.	data collected

> data tables
> graphs
> photos or drawings

_____	j.	conclusions and findings
_____	k.	glossary of terms
_____	l.	references

Display Checklist

Prepare your display to accompany the report. A good display should include the following:

Freestanding Display

_____ a.   freestanding cardboard back
_____ b.   title of experiment
_____ c.   your name
_____ d.   hypothesis
_____ e.   findings of the experiment
_____ f.   photo or illustrations of equipment
_____ g.   data tables or graphs

Additional Display Items

_____ h.   a copy of the write-up
_____ i.   actual lab equipment setup

Glossary & Index

Glossary

Atmosphere

This is comprised of the gases surrounding a planet. In the case of the Earth, the gases are primarily nitrogen and oxygen and the atmosphere is about 100 miles high. The moon has no atmosphere, and neither does Mercury, but Venus is covered in a thick fog of carbon dioxide and sulfuric acid.

Atmospheric pressure

The amount of pressure exerted by the gases in the atmosphere on an object on the surface of a planet. Again, with the Earth, the air pressure at sea level is roughly 14.7 pounds per square inch.

Aurora borealis

An atmospheric phenomenon that is created when charged particles from the sun enter the Earth's atmosphere at either the North or South Poles and burn up. When they ignite, the evening sky dances with curtains of color.

Black holes

The remnants of massive stars that have exploded and collapsed into a very dense mass of matter that has such a strong gravitational pull that even light cannot escape.

Condensation

The changing of water from the gas to the liquid phase. Condensation produces fog, clouds, and dew, to name a few things.

Constellations

An arbitrary 2-dimensional collection of stars, as seen from Earth or an Earth-orbiting observatory.

Glossary

Convective zone
With respect to the sun, the convective zone is the region of the sun or any other star that is just under the photosphere. It is composed of supergranules, or convective regions that radiate the Earth's heat out onto the surface of the sun.

Craters
Large, circular impressions left on the surface of planets and moons, which are typically created by meteors.

Diffraction grating
A piece of plastic that has had thousands of small vertical cuts made in it. When a source of light is viewed using this instrument, it allows the viewer to see the chemical fingerprint for a compound.

Earth
The third planet from the sun in our solar system, this is the only planet known to support life.

Electromagnetic spectrum
The spectrum of rays produced by stars. These waves, or rays, start with the fastest, smallest waves, gamma rays, and go on up through radio waves, which are very long.

Evaporation
This is the first step in the water cycle, where water molecules absorb energy to change state from liquid to gas. When this happens, the gas molecules rise up into the atmosphere.

Gamma rays
The smallest, fastest rays produced by the stars. Gamma rays are usually released as a by-product of a nuclear reaction or explosion.

Glossary

Greenhouse effect
This is the trapping of heat by a layer of insulating material. In the case of a greenhouse, it is a pane of plastic or glass. In the case of a planet, it is a layer of gases, usually carbon dioxide.

Infrared rays
These are rays that are typically associated with the production of heat. They are a little bit longer than visible light rays.

Jupiter
This is the largest planet in the solar system. It has at least 18 moons and a giant storm, called a red spot, that circles the planet.

Light year
This is the distance that light can travel in one year, which is a long way at 186,000 miles per second—the speed of light.

Magnetic field
This is an invisible field that is created by the magnetic core of a planet, moon, or star. It radiates out from the planet, in some cases millions of miles, and affects things like compasses and charged particles surfing the solar wind.

Magnitude
   absolute
   apparent

There are two ways that the brightness of a star is measured. One is the apparent magnitude, which is how bright the star actually looks when you are standing on the surface of the Earth. The other is the absolute magnitude, which is actually a comparison of the true luminosity or brightness of a star.

Glossary

Mars
Mars is the fourth planet in the solar system, named for the God of War. It has two moons that are believed to have once been asteroids, and an atmosphere that is not very hospitable.

Mercury
The first planet in the solar system, Mercury is very small, orbits the sun in 88 days, and gets quite toasty during the day.

Moon
The moon is a solid object that orbits a planet with a high degree of regularity. Earth has one moon, as does Pluto; the gas giants have 10 to 18 moons, depending on which giant you visit.

Neptune
The eighth planet in the solar system, Neptune has a blue appearance from space, due to the frozen methane in its atmosphere. It has an internal source of heat because it radiates two and half times as much heat as it absorbs from the sun.

Optical light rays
These account for a very thin portion of the electromagnetic spectrum. This is the portion of the spectrum that we see with our naked eyes, and it has a wavelength of between 360 and 700 nanometers.

Pluto
The last planet in the solar system, Pluto is farthest from the sun, is tied at the hip with its moon, Charon, and has an irregular orbit that is tilted 17 degrees off-center.

Precession
The tilt of a planet that creates the seasons on Earth and variations in temperatures on other planets.

Glossary

Precipitation
Precipitation makes up the third step in the water cycle. On Earth, we see this as rain, snow, freezing rain, hail, or sleet.

Radiant energy
The energy that is produced by the sun and other stars and is radiated out into the universe.

Radio waves
The longest waves in the electromagnetic spectrum.

Radiometer
A partially evacuated glass sphere that contains a set of four two-sided vanes that are silvered on one side apiece. When the radiometer is placed in the sun where infrared energy is present, it will spin.

Saturn
The gas planet that is noted for its large ring system, Saturn is the sixth planet from the sun and has many moons as well as rings.

Solar eclipse
An alignment of the sun, moon, and Earth, where the moon comes between the Earth and sun to cast a shadow on the surface of the Earth.

Spectroscope
An instrument that collects and separates light into colored bands. Each sequence of colored bands is unique and can be used as a fingerprint to identify the compounds present in a light sample.

Glossary

Star classification

Stars are classified by temperature, which in turn is indicated by color. The hottest stars are blue. As they get cooler, they're indicated by white, yellow, orange, and finally, red (for the coolest).

Ultraviolet rays

Another portion of the electromagnetic spectrum, just on the faster side of visible light, ultraviolet rays move a little bit faster than light and are the rays that we are concerned about in terms of causing skin damage.

Uranus

This is the seventh planet in the solar system, which is unique in that it has been tipped on its side. Its ring system is nearly vertical, and its magnetosphere is cockeyed.

Venus

The third planet in the solar system, Venus is very hot because it is covered in a layer of carbon dioxide and sulfuric acid clouds that traps the radiant energy that enters the Venusian atmosphere and keeps it there.

White light

This is the visible portion of the electromagnetic spectrum.

X-rays

These account for another portion of the electromagnetic spectrum, with waves on the smaller, tighter, faster side of the scale. X-rays move so fast that they can go right through most soft tissue. It is these rays that we use to view bones to see if they are broken or not.

Zodiac

The 12 constellations that move through the sun's ecliptic path.

Index

Index

Gamma rays, 24, 26–27, 48–49
Graphs
      bar, 208
      best fit, 209
      line, 208
      pie, 209
      types of, 208–209
Greenhouse effect, 60–62

Home-school parent, 13–14
How to use this book, 10–15
Hypothesis
      definition, 187
      sample, 194
      worksheet, 192–193

Information
      building a research foundation, 197–199
      gathering, 195
Infrared rays, 24, 26–27, 33–41
Iron oxide, 66

Jupiter, 72–75

Lab materials
      acquiring, 201
      sources for, 19
Light year, 160–161
Lightning, 74

Index

Index

Index

Notes

Notes

Galactic Cookie Dough • B. K. Hixson

Notes

Notes

Notes

Notes

Galactic Cookie Dough • B. K. Hixson

Notes

Notes

Notes

Notes

Galactic Cookie Dough • B. K. Hixson

Notes

Notes

Galactic Cookie Dough • B. K. Hixson

More Science Books

Thermodynamic Thrills
50 hands-on lab activities that investigate heat via conduction, convection, radiation, specific heat, and temperature.

Dig It!
50 hands-on lab activities that delve into the world of rock and mineral identification. Igneous, sedimentary, and metamorphic rocks at your rock hammer!

Newton Take 3
50 hands-on lab activities that explore the world of mechanics, forces, gravity, and Newton's three laws of motion.

Le Boom du Jour
50 more hands-on lab activities from the world of chemistry. Learn about polymers, pH, electrochemistry, and the occasional rapid oxidation.

50 Science Zingers
50 hands-on lab activities that are collected from all areas of physics and chemistry, presented in a format where you have to figure out what happens and why.

Anatomy Academy
50 hands-on lab activities that delve into the inner workings of the human body. Head to toe, inside to outside, we have you covered.

Notes